RETURN EMIGRANTS IN KERALA:
WELFARE, REHABILITATION AND DEVELOPMENT

Return Emigrants in Kerala

Welfare, Rehabilitation and Development

K.C. Zachariah
P.R. Gopinathan Nair
S. Irudaya Rajan

IDPAD

MANOHAR
2006

First published 2006

ISBN 81-7304-675-1

Published by

Ajay Kumar Jain for
Manohar Publishers & Distributors
4753/23 Ansari Road, Daryaganj
New Delhi 110 002

Typeset at

Digigrafics
New Delhi 110 049

Printed at

Lordson Publishers Pvt. Ltd.
Delhi 110 007

Distributed in South Asia by

FOUNDATION BOOKS

4381/4, Ansari Road
Daryaganj, New Delhi 110 002
and its branches at Mumbai, Hyderabad,
Bangalore, Chennai, Kolkata

Contents

Introduction

The emigration phenomenon to the Gulf has been undergoing rapid changes in terms of size of flows of manpower and money, conditions of work, job skills and experience acquired abroad. The magnitude of return flows increased during the 1990s particularly after the Kuwait war (Zachariah, Mathew and Irudaya Rajan, 1999). In 1998, there were around 7,40,000 return emigrants in the state as a whole. This study makes an in depth investigation of households of return emigrants, particularly those whose emigration and return have been comparatively recent. These recent emigrants differ from the earlier ones with respect to terms and conditions of recruitment, employment and salary as well as duration of stay abroad due to a variety of factors such as completion of the phase of infrastructural development in the Gulf countries, increased competition from other Asian countries, strengthening of the Arabization process, and the outbreak of political turmoil and hostilities in the Gulf region.

Data were obtained from return emigrants on the emigration and post-return experiences and their problems of rehabilitation and development.

Objectives

The major objective of this study is to shed light on the formulation of a policy designed to reabsorb and rehabilitate return emigrants and to utilize their investment potential and skills for the development of the state by involving than in the ongoing programme of people's planning and development.

The specific objectives include:

1. To prepare a human resources profile of return emigrants.
2. To assess the process of reabsorption of return emigrants, by comparing the economic activities of return migrants

before and after migration according to the length of time after return.

3. To obtain first-hand knowledge of their travails in the Gulf and the problems faced by them after returning to Kerala.
4. To study the investment potential and job experience of return emigrants.
5. To evaluate the policies adopted by the state government that serve the interests of return migrants.

METHOD

The sample comprised households of return emigrants and of emigrants already identified in the study conducted in 1998 (Zachariah, Mathew and Irudaya Rajan, 1999) in nine out of the fourteen districts of Kerala. The districts covered were Thiruvananthapuram, Kollam, Pathanamthitta, Alappuzha, Ernakulam, Thrissur, Palakkad, Malappuram and Kozhikode, which together accounted for nearly 80 per cent of return emigrants identified in all the fourteen districts in 1998.

A structured questionnaire (see Appendix I) covering the various areas of enquiry was used to obtain information on household characteristics, personal characteristics of return emigrants, the pre-emigration phase of return emigrants, cost and financing of emigration, and the post-return phase.

Discussions were held with the planning authorities and officials of various *Videsa Malayalee* Associations (Associations of Returned Emigrants) in Kerala on the policies and programmes for the rehabilitation of return emigrants taking into consideration the problems of their households and utilization of their development potential.

This book is divided into 8 chapters. Chapter 1 provides a review of return emigration studies with special emphasis on studies done in Kerala. A profile of return emigrants according to the 2001 survey (covering details of the year of their return, the countries in which they had been employed, age profiles, marital status, religious composition, educational status, length of service abroad and income and employment status) is presented in the next chapter. The characteristics of return emigrants in terms their households in Kerala and their comparative position in relation to return outmigrants are discussed in detail in a subsequent chapter. This is followed by a discussion of the changing profile of return emigrants vis-à-vis their pre-emigration status in terms of marital status, employment and income levels, emigration costs incurred and adjustment problems they faced while abroad. The transitions in their economic activity beginning from the pre-emigration phase to the post-return phase are examined in depth in chapter 5. The objectives which motivated them to emigrate, the costs incurred, the conditions under which they emigrated and the reasons for their return are looked into in the next chapter. Questions regarding rehabilitation and utilization of their resources for the development of Kerala's economy are discussed in chapter 7. A summary of the discussions and the conclusions and recommendations that follow are presented in the last chapter.

CHAPTER 1

Return Emigration Studies: A Review

Studies based on information collected from return migrants on the problems of their rehabilitation and realizing their development potential began to attract the attention of researchers only from the 1960s (King, 1986). Several studies have been conducted since then and most of than have to used on return emigrants from the highly developed countries of Europe and North America to their homelands in the less developed regions of Mezzogiorno (the Mediterranean countries comprising Southern Italy, Portugal and Greece), South America and the Caribbean islands (Appleyard, 1989; King, 1986). Historically speaking, emigration has been of three types: among developed countries, from developed to developing countries and from developing to developed countries (Ghosh ed., 2000). The last type was the most numerous and important. In the past, return migration was optional and migrants had the opportunity to settle down permanently in the host countries. These conditions still persist though in recent times an increasing number of host countries tent to encourage return migration especially return of 'guest workers'. For example, since 1975 France has promoted return migration of workers from Senegal to their homeland; Germany passed the Return Promotion Act in 1984 under which it promotes the return of Turkish workers. At the other end, there are migrant sending countries such as Jamaica which have implemented a vigorous programme of encouraging the return of their overseas residents with a view to making available their human and financial capital for development (UNFPA, 1998).

Some studies have examined return migration from the point of view of the host country (Reyes, 1997). In general, return migration was optional; and it assumed large dimensions only under exceptional circumstances in the host countries such as acute economic depression, natural disasters, ethnic violence or political conflicts and hostilities.

The nature of international migration assumed a new dimension with the emergence of temporary emigration of contract workers from South and South-East Asian countries since the early 1970s to the countries of the Middle East consequent on the oil price hike. Interestingly, the oil price hike had led to recession in Europe and accelerated the return flow of Senegalian, Turkish and Mediterranean workers from France and Germany. On the other hand, in the Arab world, job opportunities increased exponentially as the oil-producing countries of the region hearing invested their petro-dollars in infrastructural development schemes and to promote the growth and diversification of their economies.

Several studies based on return migration data have reconstructed the entire gamut of emigration-related activities and the costs and returns involved in each phase, from pre-emigration to post-return. For example, studies carried out in seven Asian countries during the mid-1980s under the auspices of the UN University, Tokyo (Gunatilleke ed., 1991). The typical characteristic which distinguishes migration of contract workers to the countries in the Middle East is that it is temporary and return migration is not uncertain.

Return migration studies are fraught with difficulties, both conceptual and empirical, for instance, the definition of the term itself. Return is sometimes distinguished from repatriation which is an involuntary act on the part of the migrant, forced on him by natural or political events. Emigration which results in domicile in the host country does not normally lead to permanent return. In this context, the distinction between permanent emigrants, sojourners and birds of passage may facilitate understanding of the various types of emigration (King, 1986).

In the case of temporary migration, the first migration episode is completed with return; but it need not constitute the end of the migration cycle of the person concerned. The migrant may re-emigrate to the same or a different destination. These repetitive movements are designated as 're-migration', 'second-time migration' or 'cyclical migration'. The question that arises in this context is whether one should consider as returnees only those persons who have completed their migration episodes and have returned home for good or all persons who have returned at any point of time irrespective of their plans to re-migrate. This question cannot be answered without reference to the purpose for which the study is designed.

Return migrants do not constitute a homogenous group. They differ in terms of various characteristics such as age, sex, education, experience, skills, health, residence and pre-migration status. They may also differ in terms of motivation and return and the underlying factors. For example, some scholars have focused on a disappointment theory which states that persons return because they have 'failed' (to find employment or earn expected wages) at the destination. Another type of migration is cyclical in which a wide variety of short term and repetitive onward and return movements are involved. Some authors have discussed a target income theory which describes onward migration with definite ideas about the amount of savings to be accumulated for fulfilling predetermined goals. The earlier the targeted amount is accumulated, the faster the migrants return home. Another theory is the social network theory which emphasizes that migration tends to feed back on itself through social channels and that after a critical stage is reached in the sending country, it increases the likelihood of subsequent migration (Reyes, 1997). In the light of this discussion, it is clear that migrants should be classified not only on the basis of their socio-economic, demographic and cultural characteristics, but also on the stages of social networking.

Migrant sending countries differ in their socio-economic and political set-ups. While a few countries may follow the path of central economic planning, others—which constitute the majority—may adopt a democratic set-up, with micro level decision-making under market conditions, and with varying shades of a 'mixed economy'. In planned economies, emigrants as well return migrants are determined by plan and do not cause problems of utilization of remittance incomes, nor of rehabilitation of return migrants. For example, though not a totally planned economy, South Korea has streamlined its policy regarding terms and conditions of work of its citizens in Arab countries. South Korea's public sector companies permit employees to work abroad on projects on a contract basis. In other migrant sending countries of South and South-East Asia such government managed international migration policies are rare, most migration flows take place autonomously, as dictated by market signals and political conditions at home and abroad. Return migration in such societies may give rise to problems of reabsorption and rehabilitation; but the intensity of the problem would vary, other conditions being the same, positively with the length of employment abroad and inversely with the intensity of contacts with family, relatives and friends back home. Migrants who make visits home frequent, are not accompanied by their families, and maintain regular correspondence and financial relations with their family, may find return and reabsorption easy and smooth.

Unlike countries like Jamaica which welcome return migration as a promoter of growth, migrant sending countries of South and South-East Asia, whose semi-skilled and unskilled workers are employed on a contract basis in the Gulf countries, view return migration with disfavour. Return migration implies in this case a drying up of the source of foreign remittances and increasing pressures on the job market which is plagued by massive problems of unemployment. Further, return migration may unleash problems of welfare of return migrants and their families.

Several studies on return migration have examined the phenomenon from a development perspective, irrespective of the attitude of the governments concerned towards it. The questions asked pertain to the utilization of savings and skills for the development of the regional economy; seldom have studies focused on issues like the rehabilitation of the returnees or the welfare of their households. It is often assumed that the returnees have savings, they possess skills which they would be able to utilize themselves once they return home and they would find opportunities for employment or investment. Most studies have, however, concluded that the contribution of return migrants to the economic growth of their native places is insignificant.

A study done in 1987 on behalf of UNDP/ILO-ARTEP provides a succinct account of the issues related to the settlement of return migrants in the migrant sending countries of Asia (Azam, 1987). Azam observed that the average return migrant was relatively young (between 30 and 35 years of age), had acquired technical skills and experience abroad and was desirous of improving his/her socio-economic status in the native place. Returnees who were engaged in semi-skilled and unskilled services and clerical occupations and were interested in making investments, opted for small-scale businesses, usually on a self-employment basis, in areas in which they had proficiency and experience; a few set-up grocery stores or eateries or became operators of vehicles such as buses or taxis. Persons with more savings opted for the real estate business. The group which could have entered into business—their number is extremely small—is that of professionals and businessmen who were well-educated, urban-based and had huge savings. However, factors like risk aversion and lack of business experience compelled them to avoid making long-term investments; instead they engaged in real estate transactions which offered quick and assured returns.

Azam noted that the problems faced by return migrants who sought employment included lack of appropriate skills, lack of employment opportunities in which their acquired skills could be utilized, prevailing labour market conditions, and their occupational status during the pre-emigration phase. Most of the migrant sending countries have chronic unemployment; therefore return migrants seeking employment would spell disaster for the unemployed already clamouring jobs. There is natural resistance from the latter to any preferential treatment for the former. Several skills acquired abroad are not utilized not only because of low levels of technology in use in the home country, but also because of their lack of information of available opportunities as there is no adequate mechanism for dissemination of information.

For certain groups of return migrants such as office workers, professionals and technicians who had taken leave from their organization to go abroad, reabsorption into employment may be smooth; but for other migrants employment may be possible only at the cost of others losing their jobs. The longer the time taken for the return migrant to find a job or other source of income, the more his savings would be utilized for subsistence.

Unskilled workers, including those who were engaged in skilled jobs earlier but had lost their skills because of being employed in unskilled jobs for long periods while abroad, face severe problems of finding work particularly if they seek only skilled jobs. Azam's typology of return migrants applies to a large extent to the Kerala situation.

RETURN MIGRATION STUDIES IN KERALA

In 1978 there was a spate of micro level studies on emigration in Kerala (Mathew and Gopinathan Nair, 1978; Prakash, 1978; Commerce Research Bureau, 1978; Kurien, 1978). In general, these studies examined the patterns of emigration, characteristics of the households of emigrants, and inward remittances and their impacts. Return migration was not a major concern at that point of time in Kerala because till the early 1980s emigrants could remain in the Gulf countries for as long as they wished and earn a living. Return migration emerged as a noticeable phenomenon by the mid-1980s. Earlier, the United Nations University (UNU), Tokyo had adopted the methodology of conducting studies on international migration on the basis of data collected from return migrants since they had passed through all the stages of the migration process. Of the seven country studies commissioned by the UNU in 1987, the study on India was confined to Kerala, the other studies were on the Philippines, South Korea, Thailand, Bangladesh, Sri Lanka and Pakistan.

The UNU study on Kerala was conducted during 1985 by Nair (Nair cited in Gunatilleke, 1991). On the basis of a field survey of 696 return migrants, selected on the basis of a systematic stratified random sampling technique, he found that in 1984, the proportion of return emigrants to the total number of emigrants from Kerala to the Gulf countries was 23.5 per cent. The erstwhile agricultural slave castes and the hill tribes seldom emigrated because of paucity of resources and contacts. Hindus who accounted for 60 per cent and Christians for nearly 20 per cent of the population were underrepresented among emigrants to the Gulf region. On the other hand, Muslims who formed about 20 per cent of the population constituted 78 per cent of the Gulf emigrants. In his survey, Nair did not find any women respondents.

Nair discussed the marital, educational, employment and income status of return emigrants during their pre-emigration phase, the process of emigration and the costs incurred, the conditions of employment abroad and the reasons for return. Most of the respondents belonged to relatively large households, were unmarried and below 30 years of age on the eve of their first emigration. Two-thirds of them had emigrated on the basis of informed arrangements without formal contracts with the prospective employers. In the absence of formal contracts or any idea of the types of employment available, there was total uncertainty about wages or salaries. Only about 13 per cent had jobs which they found satisfying. The average cost incurred by the respondents on passport, visa, medical check-up and air fare was Rs. 9,000. The amount varied from less than Rs. 5,000 in a few cases to Rs. 50,000 in a significant proportion. Such inordinate variations were due to the unregulated and uncontrolled nature of the emigration process. There were many fraudulent agencies and individuals thriving in the emigration business. Nearly two-fifths of the respondents had to borrow money to meet the costs incurred. Surprisingly, even in the absence of a guarantee of getting employment, most of the respondents found jobs without having to wait for long periods. Working and living conditions in the host countries were not unfavourable according to the majority of them. Marital relations remained intact in the case of four-fifths of them, a fact which contradicted the media hype that most young wives of 'hasty love marriages' committed adultery. The emigrants adjusted admirably well to the foreign environment, though most of them were under severe strains of adjustment.

A few of return emigrants, had as many as five different jobs in succession before returning to Kerala. Most of the respondents restricted their expenses with a view to remitting their savings home. The proportion of savings to income increased by the level of income. The bulk of the transferred savings (remittances) was used by the recipient households on routine consumption items. Despite this, they had substantial amounts left which they used for a variety of purposes such as acquisition or improvement of land, construction or renovation of houses, purchase of vehicles, ornaments and consumer durables, investments in financial assets, repayment of loans and marriages of children. The average amount spent on these items per recipient household was Rs. 79,000.

Most of the respondents reported that their socio-economic status and asset position had improved. Household consumption levels had also significantly increased. However, almost 15 per cent of the respondents had experienced failure.

For over three-fourths of the respondents, returning to Kerala was not optional; for the remaining, return was necessitated by difficult working conditions abroad or problems in their households in Kerala. Thus, a vast majority had returned against their will, or before they had achieved their targets. Those who had returned voluntarily were relatively well qualified with professional, technical, managerial and administrative credentials. In the post-return phase, less than 2 per cent had opted for retirement from work. About 15 per cent had found various types of employment and nearly one-fourth were engaged in self-employment programmes. The vast majority (60 per cent) remained unemployed and sought jobs in Kerala or abroad. At the time of this study, organizations of return migrants had begun to emerge and their main agenda was to pressurize the state government for placement in jobs or for assistance in setting up a business. The few who had sizeable savings were reluctant to invest their funds in Kerala for a variety of reasons such as labour militancy, raw material shortages, lack of technical competence, undue government interventions and marketing problems.

Information on the number of return migrants in Kerala was not available till 1986. In that year, the government conducted a survey and arrived at a figure of 865,000 (GOK, 1987). In 1992-3, another survey conducted by the government noted that the number of return migrants was 125,000 (GOK, 1994). These surveys broadly corroborated the findings of the study by Nair, in terms of consumption patterns, post-return employment status, etc.

The volume of return migration suddenly increased during 1990 consequent on the outbreak of the Kuwait–Iraq war; nearly 80,000 Keralites were repatriated from Kuwait. The war sent shock waves in the state administration and the situation was considered to have the 'potentiality of posing fundamental problems in the region' (Saith, 1992). It was feared that these migrants would add to the live register of employment exchanges and swell the ranks of the unemployed in the state by at least about 50,000 persons and between 50,000 and 70,000 households would be rendered destitute. The total loss of remittances to the state was estimated to be of the order of about 1.0 to 1.5 per cent of the state's domestic product. For the government, the immediate rehabilitation of repatriates of such a magnitude was well-nigh impossible. It was feared that there would be adverse impacts on the banking sector, consumption expenditure, construction activities, trade, transport and business in general. The spectre of unfinished houses and homeless return migrants, of indigent persons and families deprived of their succour and support, and school children deprived of schooling loomed large in Kerala (Saith, 1992). The state government panicked, but it was not in a position to take any effective step to meet the crisis. Fortunately for the repatriates and for Kerala's economy, the Gulf war came to an end and most of the repatriates returned to their earlier jobs in Kuwait. A survey conducted by the government in 1992-3 reported that only 9 per cent of the war repatriates from Kuwait had stayed back in Kerala, they were either uninterested in re-emigration or were not able to go back for other reasons (GOK, 1994). It was also found that the proportion of self-employed was 32 per cent and the proportion of unemployed was 21 per cent. A study by Issac noted that there were several persons among them who were poor, unskilled and sick, including a few women who could not re-emigrate and were thus left in the lurch (Issac, 1993).

A study of 355 return migrants registered with the cell in the government secretariat constituted in the aftermath of the Kuwait–Iraq war, was done by Nambiar (1998). He found that more than three-fourths of return migrants had gone back involuntarily for reasons such as expiry and cancellation of visa, repatriation and deportation; their situation could be described as migration failure. Among the returnees nearly 53 per cent were employed, 42 per cent were unemployed and the rest had retired from the labour force. Of the employed, 45 per cent were self-employed, and the rest were employed as casual or permanent workers in the private sector. Only 1 per cent had found government jobs.

In recent years, another type of return migration has been seen which is known in Kerala as 'amnesty return'. The Gulf countries have been flooded with several thousands Asians who had sneaked into these countries without valid passports, visas or work permits.

The UAE launched a process of repatriating the illegal immigrants after granting them amnesty for illegal entry and stay. Nearly 45,000 persons were compulsorily repatriated to India in 1996, of these around 20,000-25,000 were Keralites. As was the case in 1990, in 1996 also the Government of India (and the Kerala government) made arrangements for the return of 'amnesty' migrants. Among the salient features of the amnesty returnees as revealed by an analysis of the answers provided by 10,874 persons from among them were: women formed only a miniscule proportion of 0.3 per cent; about 55 per cent were married; the majority were in the prime working age group of 30-40 years; Muslims constituted 53 per cent, Hindus 42 per cent and Christians 3 per cent; educational levels were low, 80 per cent were not even matriculates. All of them had worked in the host countries during intermittent periods as unskilled labour in households, industries and construction sites under hazardous conditions for paltry wages. Their households remained poverty-striken both during their stay abroad and after their return. Other countries of the Gulf region have also adopted the policy of compulsory repatriation of illegal immigrants (Nair, 1999). In a survey of 300 return migrants in Thiruvananthapuram conducted in December 1997, Nair observed that the profile of return migrants had by and large remained unchanged—low educational qualifications, return by compulsion, poor familial background, unskilled and semi-skilled jobs abroad, high rates of self-employed in the post-return phase and low levels of savings in general with a few isolated cases of high savers. The major difference observed from the earlier studies was that women constituted about one-sixth of the sample, and one-sixth of men and nearly half of the women were unemployed (Nair, 1999).

By far the most comprehensive studies on migration in Kerala covering both migration within India and international migration are those by Zachariah, Mathew and Irudaya Rajan (1999; 2000; 2001a; 2001b; Zachariah and Irudaya Rajan (2001a; 2001b) examined the profiles of return migrants and their socio-economic status in the post-return phase. However, with a view to reconstructing the entire migration cycle from a sample of migrants who had completed the process to examining in detail the problems and possibilities of their rehabilitation and releasing their development potential, a new study was found necessary. Hence, this present exercise. It is expected that this study would suggest a package of policy prescriptions which have a bearing on rehabilitation, welfare and development of return emigrants in Kerala.

II

KERALA MIGRATION STUDY, 1998

Conducted in 1998, this study aimed to examine all aspects of migration from Kerala, internal and external, and outward and inward migration. All the selected households were asked the following questions:

Has any member of this household who is now its usual member ever lived outside India for a year or more?
Has any member of this household who is now its usual member ever lived outside India for periods of less than one year for the purpose of studies or in search of jobs?

These questions identified return emigrants in the household (see appendix II).

RETURN EMIGRANTS IN KERALA, 1998

The number of return emigrants in Kerala in 1998 was estimated at 7,39,000. For every 100 households there were 11.6 return emigrants and for every 100 persons there were 2.36 return emigrants.

Return emigrants were unevenly distributed in the districts. The number and rate of return emigrants was highest in Malappuram district and lowest in the two hilly districts of Wayanad and Idukki. The magnitude of return emigrants is presented in Table 1.1.

Among the 61 talukas, Thiruvananthapuram had the highest number of return emigrants, i.e. around 50,000. However, with respect to the rate of return emigrants, Kodungallur taluka ranked first with 39 return emigrants for every 100 households followed by Chirayinkeezhu taluka with 28 return emigrants (Table 1.2).

TABLE 1.1: RETURN MIGRANTS IN KERALA, 1998

Districts	*REM*	*REM/100 HH*
Malappuram	1,23,750	20.5
Trivandrum	1,18,878	18.1
Thrissur	1,16,788	18.6
Kollam	74,106	13.2
Kozhikode	60,910	11.5
Pathanamthitta	54,537	18.5
Ernakulam	45,028	7.4
Palakkad	39,234	7.4
Alappuzha	34,572	7.2
Kannur	28,263	6.1
Kottayam	18,164	4.6
Kasaragod	16,667	8.2
Idukki	5,017	2.0
Wayanad	3,327	2.1
Kerala	7,39,245	11.6

Source: Zachariah, Mathew and Irudaya Rajan, 2003.

The centre of location (COL) of return emigrants was somewhere in Kothamangalam taluka in Idukki district while the COL of emigrants from Kerala was in Alwaye taluk in Ernakulam

TABLE 1.2: TALUK OF RESIDENCE OF RETURN EMIGRANTS (TALUKAS WITH 20,000 OR MORE RETURN EMIGRANTS)

	REM	*REM/100 HH*
Trivandrum	49,618	24.7
Ernad	48,097	18.9
Kollam	40,310	20.4
Chirayinkeezhu	37,595	27.6
Thirur	36,763	18.6
Kodungallur	26,617	38.6
Mukundapuram	24,433	13.8
Thalapally	24,865	21.1
Chavakkad	24,786	26.4
Neyattum kara	22,825	13.4
Quilandy	21,941	16.0
Vadakara	21,114	17.9
Total	7,93,245	11.6

Source: Zachariah, Mathew and Irudaya Rajan, 2003.

TABLE 1.3: COUNTRY OF ORIGIN OF RETURN EMIGRANTS

Country of Origin	%	*Frequency*
Saudi Arabia	41.2	3,04,395
United Arab Emirates	26.0	1,92,926
Muscat	9.9	73,496
Bahrain	6.0	44,097
Kuwait	4.7	34,910
Qatar	3.1	23,274
Oman	2.1	15,312
South-East Asia	1.1	7,962
Iraq, Iran	0.7	4,900
Nepal, Bangladesh	0.7	4,900
Africa	0.5	3,675
USA	0.2	1,225
Europe	0.1	612
Others	3.7	27,561
Total	100.0	7,39,245

Source: Zachariah, Mathew and Irudaya Rajan, 2003.

district. Return emigrants tended to settle down south of the place to which they originally belonged.

As return emigration is the result of past emigration, the origin of the former should follow the pattern of destination of the latter. The largest proportion of return emigrants were from Saudi Arabia (41 per cent) followed by the United Arab Emirates (26 per cent). The full distribution is given in Table 1.3.

The number of return emigrants in recent years far exceeded those who had returned in earlier years. For example, 1,27,000 emigrants returned in 1997 compared to only 43,000 in 1992 (Table 1.4). This is indicative of an increasing trend in return emigration. But this presents an exaggerated picture of the recent return of emigrants as the earlier numbers were subject to attrition due to deaths and re-emigration.

Demographic Characteristics of Return Emigrants

Nearly 90 per cent of return emigrants in Kerala in 1998 were married males (Table 1.5). A majority of them were middle aged. More than one-third were in the 30-9 years age group (Figure 1.1).

TABLE 1.4: RETURN EMIGRANTS BY YEAR OF RETURN

Year	*Return Emigrants (in thousands)*
1997	127
1996	107
1995	73
1994	58
1993	35
1992	43
1991	20
1990	37
1993-7	400
1988-92	147
1983-7	69
Total	739*

Note: * Including return emigrants who came back before 1983 and during the first five months of 1998.

Source: Zachariah, Mathew and Irudaya Rajan, 2003.

TABLE 1.5: SEX COMPOSITION OF RETURN EMIGRANTS

	Total	%
Males	6,59,261	89.2
Females	79,984	10.8
Total	7,39,245	100.0

Source: Zachariah, Mathew and Irudaya Rajan, 2003.

The average age of return emigrants in 1998 was 40 years (Table 1.6). Thus, a typical return emigrant was a married man in his 30s (Table 1.7).

TABLE 1.6: AGE COMPOSITION OF RETURN EMIGRANTS

Below 20	5.4
20-9	17.1
30-9	33.7
40-9	27.1
50-9	11.5
60-9	3.5
70+	1.8
Total	100.0

Source: Zachariah, Mathew and Irudaya Rajan, 2003.

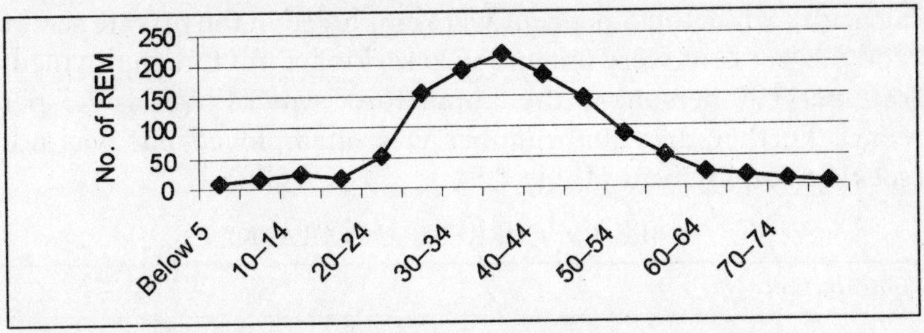

Source: Zachariah, Mathew and Irudaya Rajan, 2003.

FIGURE 1.1: RETURN EMIGRANTS BY AGE

TABLE 1.7: MARITAL STATUS COMPOSITION

Marital Status	%
Single	9.9
Married	88.2
Widowed	1.1
Divorced	0.2
Separated	0.7
Total	100.0

Source: Zachariah, Mathew and Irudaya Rajan, 2003.

Educational Attainment

Return emigrants were not highly educated as a little over 10 per cent of them had below primary level of education. Only around 6 per cent had a degree (Table 1.8).

Nearly two-fifths of return emigrants were self-employed. Over one-fourth (26 per cent) were engaged as labourers in the non-

TABLE 1.8: EDUCATIONAL ATTAINMENT

Education	%
Below Primary	10.2
Primary	19.4
Below Secondary	39.5
Secondary	24.8
Degree	6.1
Total	100.0

Source: Zachariah, Mathew and Irudaya Rajan, 2003.

agricultural sector, 5 per cent were employed in the private sector and 6.6 per cent were unemployed seeking a job (unemployment rate per 100 persons in the labour force was as high as 7.5 per cent). Further, an equal number was unemployed but was not seeking employment (Table 1.9).

TABLE 1.9: CURRENT OCCUPATION

Occupation	%
Government Employment	2.2
Semi-government	0.3
Private Sector	5.4
Self-employment	37.8
Unpaid Worker	1.5
Agricultural Labour	4.3
Non-agricultural Labour	26.0
Unemployed	6.6
Unemployed not Seeking Job	6.4
Student	2.1
Household Work	6.9
Pensioners	0.4
Total	100.0

Source: Zachariah, Mathew and Irudaya Rajan, 2003.

RETURN EMIGRANTS BY COMMUNITY

A little over 45 per cent of return emigrants in 1998 were Muslims, Ezhavas comprised about 19 per cent, Syrian Christians and

TABLE 1.10: RETURN EMIGRANTS BY COMMUNITY, 1998

	%	
	Rem	*Emi*
SC/ST	1.7	1.4
Nairs	7.0	7.7
Ezhavas	19.1	13.1
Syrian Christians	10.4	11.7
Latin Christians	10.5	8.1
Muslims	45.3	50.7
Others	6.0	7.3
Total	100.0	100.0

Source: Zachariah, Mathew and Irudaya Rajan, 2003.

Latin Christians were more or less equal, around 10 per cent each. Compared with the proportion of emigrants, the number of return emigrants was higher among the Ezhavas, the Latin Christians and the Scheduled Castes. Their number was less in all other communities. Thus, the propensity to return was higher among the Ezhavas, the Scheduled Castes and the Latin Christians than among the other communities (Table 1.10).

CHAPTER 2

Return Emigrants: A Profile

In the present study 2,081 households were enumerated from the selected nine districts. In 1998, the number of households identified were 2,085 (see Table 2.1). These 2,081 households had a total of 11,164 members: 5,164 males and 6,000 females. The distribution of households by the number of persons per household in the two surveys is given in Table 2.2.

TABLE 2.1: NUMBER OF ELIGIBLE HOUSEHOLDS BY DISTRICTS, 1998 AND 2001

Districts	*1998**	*2001#*
Thiruvananthapuram	368	367
Kollam	201	200
Pathanamthitta	166	176
Alappuzha	117	109
Ernakulam	188	193
Thrissur	255	277
Palakkad	150	111
Malappuram	413	412
Kozhikode	227	236
Total	2,085	2,081

Notes: * Zachariah, Mathew and Irudaya Rajan, 1999.
Field survey, 2001.

There were some minor differences between the distribution in 2001 compared to that in 1998. In the interim, the proportion of smaller households (of less than 4 members) had increased and the proportion of larger households had decreased. This change is in tune with the overall trend in household size in Kerala. However, the average size of the household in the sample (5.4 persons) remained unchanged as between 1998 and 2001.

TABLE 2.2: DISTRIBUTION OF SAMPLE HOUSEHOLDS BY NUMBER OF PERSONS

No. of Persons	%	
	2001#	*1998**
1	1.7	1.6
2	6.6	6.3
3	15.8	15.3
4	21.1	21.1
5	17.0	17.9
6	11.8	12.1
7	8.1	8.5
8	5.8	5.4
9	4.2	4.1
10+	7.8	7.8
Total	100.0	100.0

Notes: * Zachariah, Mathew and Irudaya Rajan, 1999.
Field survey, 2001.

Households with Return Emigrants

However, not all the sample households had return emigrants. Of the 2,081 households, only 884 had one or more return emigrants whereas in 1998, only 922 had a return emigrant. The distribution of households by the number of return emigrants is given Table 2.3. It can be seen that the proportion of households with return emigrants decreased in the interim.

TABLE 2.3: HOUSEHOLDS BY THE NUMBER OF RETURN EMIGRANTS, 1998 AND 2001

No. of REM	*No. HHs*	
	2001#	*1998**
0	57.5	55.8
1	37.3	38.8
2	4.0	3.8
3	1.2	1.6
Total	100.0	100.0

Notes: * Zachariah, Mathew and Irudaya Rajan, 1999.
Field survey, 2001.

Categories of Return Emigrants

Return emigrants enumerated in this survey were of three types:

1. Persons who had returned before 1999.
2. Persons who had been abroad in 1998, but had returned during 1999-2001.
3. Persons who had emigrated and returned after 1998.

The majority (73.5 per cent) of return emigrants enumerated had returned before 1998 (Table 2.4). Nearly one-fifth (20.6 per cent) of return emigrants had been abroad in 1998. The percentage of new return emigrants from among those who had emigrated after the 1998 survey and had returned before the present survey was 6.

TABLE 2.4: RETURN MIGRANTS BY CATEGORY

Category	*No.*	*Per cent*
Return Emigrants of 1998 Survey*	753	73.5
Return Emigrants among Emigrants of 1998 Survey*	211	20.6
New Return Emigrants#	61	5.9
Total	1,025	100.0

Notes: * Zachariah, Mathew and Irudaya Rajan, 1999.
Field survey, 2001.

Return Migration Rate

It is difficult to calculate the return emigration rate in this study, as the households were not selected at random. In 1998, there were 1,090 return emigrants in the nine sample districts. However, in 2001, only 753 of them could be contacted. Nearly 30 per cent had either re-emigrated or moved to other areas. Similarly, in 1998 there were 1,831 emigrants living abroad; of these 211 had returned during 1998-2000. The return migration rate among them was 11.5 per cent (Table 2.5).

The distribution of return emigrants by districts showed no marked difference during 1998–2001. Mare was a slight shift towards Ernakulam and Kozhikode districts and away from Thrissur and Malappuram districts.

TABLE 2.5: RETURN EMIGRANTS BY DISTRICT

District	%	
	2001#	*1998**
Thiruvananthapuram	19.5	20.9
Kollam	9.4	9.3
Pathanamthitta	8.2	8.7
Alappuzha	5.4	4.5
Ernakulam	10.0	7.2
Thrissur	15.9	16.3
Palakkad	3.5	5.1
Malappuram	17.4	18.2
Kozhikode	10.9	9.5
Total	100.0	100.0

Notes: * Zachariah, Mathew and Irudaya Rajan, 1999.
Field survey, 2001.

Relation to Head of Household

The majority of return emigrants, i.e. more than half of the total were heads of households. Around one-fourth were married and nearly one-tenth were unmarried members of households (Table 2.6).

TABLE 2.6: RELATION OF RETURN EMIGRANTS TO HEAD

Head	51.8
Wife	4.6
Unmarried Member	11.4
Married Member	27.8
Brother/Sister	1.4
Others	3.0
Total	100.0

Source: Field survey, 2001.

Year of Return of Return Emigrants

In 1998, it was projected that the number of return emigrants would rapidly increase after 1999, that the number of return emigrants would outnumber emigrants and that the annual net emigration would become negative in the early part of the twenty-first century.

However, it was observed that the number of return emigrants did not increase as rapidly as was expected. As shown in Table 2.7, the number of return emigrants in 2001 was less than that in 1998 and the numbers for almost all years for which data are given in the table. The 1996-8 period witnessed the highest number of return emigrants compared to any preceding or succeeding year. The data for both 2001 and 1998 indicated that the number of return emigrants peaked in 1997 (see Figure 2.1). Further, there was a downward trend in the number of return emigrants. It is quite possible that some of the earlier return emigrants had re-emigrated since 1998.

TABLE 2.7: NUMBER OF RETURN EMIGRANTS BY YEAR OF RETURN (NINE DISTRICTS)

Year	*2001*#	*1998**
2001	6+	–
2000	88	–
1999	85	–
1998	101	119+
1997	118	186
1996	103	158
1995	81	113
1994	59	82
1993	33	55
1992	39	66
1991	20	30
1990	40	55
1989	20	23
1988	35	40
1987	16	16
1986	22	29
1985	12	24
1984	12	11
1983	10	23
1982	11	12
1981	7	5
1980	9	5

Notes: + For part of the year only.
* Zachariah, Mathew and Irudaya Rajan, 1999.
# Field survey, 2001.

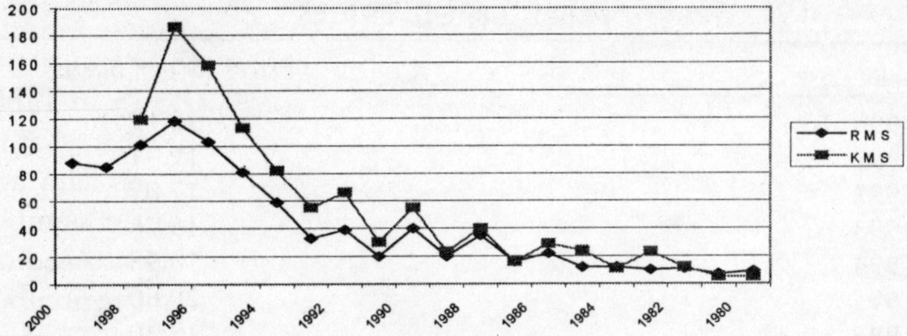

FIGURE 2.1: NUMBER OF RETURN EMIGRANTS BY YEAR OF RETURN

A partial explanation for this unexpected trend could be found in the pattern of crude oil prices. Higher oil prices may be reflected in the demand for expatriate workers in the Gulf countries. Of course, several other factors are in operation as well such as immigration policies, political conditions and economic plans (for more details, see Zachariah, Prakash and Irudaya Rajan, 2002; 2003; 2004).

As had been postulated earlier (Zachariah, Mathew and Irudaya Rajan, 1999), the past trend in emigration determines the volume of return emigration. While this postulate is true, annual fluctuations in the volume of return emigration could be affected by other factors, including changes in the price of oil. The annual prices of petroleum for the 1990-2000 periods are given in Table 2.8. It is likely that the low price of oil during 1996-8 had an adverse impact in the sense that it triggered a sudden increase in the exodus of foreign workers from the Gulf countries. When oil prices recovered dramatically after 1999, there was a sharp decline in return emigration.

In such circumstances, it would not be realistic to make any long-term predictions about the volume of annual return flows of emigrants, except that it is the volume of emigrants that eventually determines the volume of return emigration, Gulf emigration being one of contract workers. Given the rates and levels of remuneration prevalent in the Gulf countries, workers from Kerala would try to prolong their stay in those countries, though they do not allow majority of the contract workers to stay, on the average, for more than three years at a stretch.

TABLE 2.8: OIL PRICES

Year	*Prices ($ per Barrel)*
1990	20.19
1991	19.31
1992	17.07
1993	15.76
1994	16.98
1995	20.60
1996	19.20
1997	12.71
1998	17.88
1999	28.39
2000	29.50

Source: *Brent Blend Price*, weekly, 1990-2001, Statistics, Norway, 2001 (http:/www.ssb.no/emner/10/06/nos oljegass/nos c651/en/tab/t-32.html).

Destination of First Emigration

Saudi Arabia was the destination of nearly 40 per cent of return emigrants during their first emigration from Kerala. Dubai ranked next in importance which was the destination of 16 per cent of return emigrants. The other major destinations were Bahrain, Muscat, Abu Dhabi and Kuwait (Table 2.9).

TABLE 2.9: DESTINATION OF THE FIRST EMIGRATION OF RETURN EMIGRANTS

Country	%	
	First Emigration	*Last Residence*
Abu Dhabi	6.0	7.9
Dubai	16.4	12.8
Saudi Arabia	39.7	41.1
Kuwait	6.0	4.5
Muscat	9.1	12.1
Oman	3.1	3.4
Qatar	2.6	3.4
Bahrain	10.3	7.0
Sharjah	3.6	4.9
All Others	3.2	2.9
Total	100.0	100.0

Source: Field survey, 2001.

As in the case of destination of first emigration, the country of last residence before return was also Saudi Arabia for more than 40 per cent of return emigrants. The other major regions were Dubai, Muscat and Abu Dhabi.

DEMOGRAPHIC STRUCTURE OF RETURN EMIGRANTS

SEX COMPOSITION

More than 90 per cent of return emigrants in the sample were men. There was a slight increase in the proportion of male return emigrants (88.7 per cent to 91 per cent) between 1998 and 2001 (see Table 2.10).

TABLE 2.10: RETURN EMIGRANTS BY SEX, 1998 AND 2001

Sex	*Numbers*		*%*	
	2001	*1998*	*2001*	*1998*
Males	933	967	91.0	88.7
Females	92	123	9.0	11.3
Total	1,025	1,090		

Source: Field survey, 2001.

AGE DISTRIBUTION

Date pertaining to the age of return emigrants at the time of emigration, at the time of return and at the time of the present survey is given in Table 2.11. At the time of emigration, about two-thirds of the respondents were in the 20-9 years age group. At the time of return, around 70 per cent were in the 25-44 years age group, the peak being in the 30-4 years age group (20.4 per cent). At the time of the present survey, the respondents were spread across all age groups, but two-thirds of them were in the 30-49 years category.

The average age of return emigrants at the time of the survey in 2001 was 41.6 years, 30.3 years at the time of their first emigration, and 35.8 years at the time of return. Thus, the interval between emigration and return was 5.5 years and an average emigrant had been in Kerala for nearly 5.8 years after his return.

TABLE 2.11: AGE DISTRIBUTION OF RETURN EMIGRANTS IN 2001(%)

Age Group (Years)	*Age at Emigration*	*Age at Return*	*Present Age*
Less than 20	9.2	8.1	2.3
20-4	27.3	6.6	2.8
25-9	28.2	15.4	10.0
30-4	16.1	20.4	16.7
35-9	11.7	18.0	17.8
40-4	5.7	15.2	16.9
45-9	1.1	8.5	15.6
50-4	0.5	4.4	8.3
55-9	0.1	2.3	5.8
60+	0.1	1.1	3.9
Total	100.0	100.0	100.0

Source: Field survey, 2001.

Marital Status

Most of the respondents (88 per cent) were married at the time of the survey and almost 10 per cent had never married (see Table 2.12).

TABLE 2.12: MARITAL COMPOSITION OF RETURN EMIGRANTS

Marital Status	*2001*
Never Married	9.8
Married	87.8
Widowed	1.4
Divorced/Separated	1.0
Total	100.0

Source: Field survey, 2001.

Community

Muslims constituted 43 per cent of the sample and Hindus about one-third. More than half (55 per cent) of the Hindu respondents belonged to the Ezhava community. A little over one-fifth were Christian and among them three-fourths were Syrian and the remaining were Latin Christians. The number of Brahmins was almost negligible (see Table 2.13).

TABLE 2.13: DISTRIBUTION BY COMMUNITY

	%
Hindu	33.6
Muslim	43.4
Christian	21.3
Syrian	15.8
Latin	5.5
Other Non-Hindus	5.5
Hindus by sub-sectors	
SC/ST	1.5
Nair	6.8
Ezhava	18.7
Brahmin	0.1
Other Hindus	6.5
Total	33.6

Source: Field survey, 2001.

EDUCATION

Almost three-fifths of respondents' educational qualifications were below the secondary level. Around 8 per cent held a degree or higher qualifications (see Table 2.14). The average number of years of schooling of return emigrants was 7.3.

An important point to note is that the average educational level of return emigrants was lower than that of emigrants still working abroad. Return emigrants did not constitute a random

TABLE 2.14: COMPOSITION OF RETURN EMIGRANTS BY EDUCATION, 2001

Level of Education	*Per cent*
Below Primary	5.6
Primary	12.5
Below Secondary	41.3
Secondary	32.7
Degree	7.9
Total	100.0

Source: Field survey, 2001.

TABLE 2.15: EDUCATIONAL ATTAINMENT OF EMIGRANTS STILL ABROAD AND RETURN EMIGRANTS

	Emigrants %	*Return Emigrants %*
Illiterate	0.8	1.5
Literate	1.0	2.4
Below Primary	3.9	6.8
Primary	11.4	20.1
Below Secondary	43.1	38.0
Secondary	29.2	24.7
Degree	10.5	6.6
Total	100.0	100.0

Source: Zachariah, Mathew and Irudaya Rajan, 1999.

sample of all emigrants. A greater proportion of them had lower levels of education and very few were in the higher educational category. Return emigrants were under-represented in the higher educational categories such as degree and over-represented in the lower educational categories such as illiterate, literate without schooling, etc. (see Table 2.15). The average number of years of schooling was 9 in the case of emigrants and 7.3 in the case of return emigrants.

Professional and Technical Education

Information about the technical skills of return emigrants could have considerable significance from the point of their utilization in the local level development efforts in Kerala. Data on technical and professional education of return emigrants is given in Table 2.16. Only 18.7 per cent of return emigrants had technical or professional education; 12.3 per cent were certificate holders; 3.5 per cent had a diploma and 2.9 per cent had a degree. Further, 33.7 per cent had some work experience in technical trades, but did not have any formal training (Table 2.17).

Some broad conclusions may be drawn from the foregoing discussion.

1. The group of recent return emigrants had in general a low level of education.

TABLE 2.16: DISTRIBUTION BY LEVEL OF TECHNICAL AND PROFESSIONAL EDUCATION

Professional Category	*Level of Education**					
No Technical/ Professional Education	1	2	3	4	5	Total
Carpentry	27	5				32
Masonry	24	4				28
Electrician	16	11	6	2		35
Civil Engineering		7	8	7		22
Mechanical Engineering	9	7	1	2		19
Architect	2	1				3
Medicine	1	6	5	2		14
Laboratory Technician			1			1
Accountancy	1			7		8
Bookkeeping	1					1
Computer	1	3	1	2		7
Driving	76	27				103
Others	94	20	6	3		123
Total	477	337	123	35	29	1001

Notes: * 1 = no technical training or work experience; 2 = work experience without formal training; 3 = Certificate; 4 = Diploma; 5 = Degree.

Source: Field survey, 2001.

2. Those who returned belonged to the group which had relatively lower levels of education.
3. Return emigrants had lower levels of technical education as compared to those who did not return.

PERIOD OF SERVICE IN KERALA BEFORE EMIGRATION

On an average, return emigrants had been employed in Kerala for around 7.7 years before they emigrated to the Gulf countries (Table 2.18). Further, 36 per cent had between 5 and 10 years of work experience, 33 per cent had more than 10 years and 31 per cent had less than 5 years including persons without employment. In short, largely those people emigrated who had some years of work experience in Kerala before emigration.

TABLE 2.17: DISTRIBUTION OF EMIGRANTS AND RETURN EMIGRANTS BY TECHNICAL EDUCATION

Status	*Among All Migrants*		*Among Emigrants with Technical Knowledge*	
	Emigrants	*Return Emigrants*	*Emigrants*	*Return Emigrants*
	1998	*2001*	*1998*	*2001*
No Technical Knowledge	67.3	61.3		
Technical Knowledge but No Schooling	12.7	24.4	39.7	63.2
Certificate Holder	13.0	8.9	40.6	23.1
Diploma Holder	4.0	2.8	12.5	7.3
Degree Holder	2.3	2.5	7.2	6.4
Total	100.0	100.0	100.0	100.0

Source: Zachariah, Mathew and Irudaya Rajan, 1999.
Field survey, 2001.

TABLE 2.18: PERIOD OF SERVICE IN KERALA BEFORE EMIGRATION

Years	%
0-4	31.0
5-9	36.0
10-14	19.5
15-19	8.7
20+	4.8
Total	100.0

Source: Field survey, 2001.

Period of Service Abroad of Return Emigrants

Nearly two-thirds of return emigrants had worked in the Gulf countries for less than 5 years; nearly 30 per cent had worked for less than 2 years. The average length of work experience abroad for the entire group was 7 years and 3 months (Table 2.19).

Period Since Return to Kerala

On average the interval between return to Kerala and the date of the survey was 6 years. The distribution of return emigrants in

TABLE 2.19: PERIOD OF SERVICE IN THE GULF OF RETURN EMIGRANTS

Period (in Months)	%
12 or less	9.7
13-24	19.7
25-36	14.4
37-48	12.4
49-60	9.7
61-72	6.3
73-84	5.9
85-96	6.0
97-108	3.6
109-20	6.0
120+	6.3
Total	100.0

Source: Field survey, 2001.

terms of the length of time they had been in Kerala since their return is presented in Table 2.20.

TABLE 2.20: DURATION SINCE RETURN TO KERALA

Duration Since Return (years)	%
5 <	53.1
5-10	24.6
10-15	14.1
15-20	5.5
20-5	1.6
More than 25	1.1
Total	100.0

Source: Field survey, 2001.

Income from Employment before Emigration

The average annual income from employment of return emigrants before emigration was Rs. 15,080. Almost 41 per cent of them had earned less than Rs. 1,000 and over three-fourths less than Rs. 2,000 per month. The monthly income of around 6 per cent was more than Rs. 3000 (see Table 2.21).

TABLE 2.21: SALARY OF RETURN EMIGRANTS IN KERALA BEFORE EMIGRATION

Salary (Rs.)	%
Below 6,000	12.6
6,000-11,999	28.8
12,000-14,999	5.8
15,000-17,999	8.8
18,000-20,999	13.0
21,000-23,999	0.0
24,000-29,999	9.6
30,000-35,999	5.6
36,000+	5.9
Total	100.0

Source: Field survey, 2001.

Annual Income While Abroad

Return emigrants earned on an average around Rs. 1,20,000 per year when they were in the Gulf. The distribution of respondents according to income earned abroad is given in Table 2.22. There was an increase of Rs. 1,05,000 over the amount they had been earning (Rs. 15,000) before emigration. The difference was higher in the case of those who had returned in recent years.

TABLE 2.22: ANNUAL INCOME OF RETURN EMIGRANTS IN THE GULF COUNTRIES

Annual Income (Rs.)	%
Below 25,000	1.4
25,000-50,000	7.9
50,000-75,000	20.9
75,000-1,00,000	27.1
1,00,000-1,50,000	25.5
1,50,000-2,00,000	8.2
2,00,000-2,50,000	3.9
2,50,000-3,00,000	1.1
3,00,000-3,60,000	4.1
3,60,000+	4.0

Source: Field survey, 2001.

Number of Times Migrated

More than three-fourths of return emigrants had been abroad only once. However, around 14 per cent had two emigration episodes. Some had made more than five trips. The average number of times return emigrants went abroad for employment was 1.43.

Return emigrants were a selected group from among the emigrants. They had relatively lower levels of education than the emigrants still working abroad. The propensity to return was much higher among the Ezhava and the Schedule Castes than among emigrants belonging to the other communities.

CHAPTER 3

Return Outmigrants: Characteristics and Problems

INTRODUCTION

Since the early 1970s, when the Gulf countries opened up for emigrants from Kerala, for all practical purposes, migration in Kerala became synonymous with migration to the Gulf. Internal migration, i.e. migration to the other states in India, was relegated to a secondary position. Therefore, in recent years, much of the public attention was directed towards the problems of emigrants employed in the Gulf countries and their rehabilitation on their return to Kerala. NRI associations mushroomed in every nook and corner of the state to take up the cause of emigrants. Several international conferences at the government level were held to discuss the problems of Gulf Malayalis and Gulf returnees. The government launched a number of welfare projects to deal with some of the pressing problems of the Gulf returnees.

Internal migrants, those who are living outside the state but elsewhere within India, and those who have returned, believe that they have been excluded from the government's plans for rehabilitation of return migrants. It is not that the government has done nothing for them. Recently, the government organized a sort of seminar where they could express their problems. However, nothing came out of it. In fact, some of the Malayali associations in Mumbai who participated in the meetings voiced their concern over the neglect shown to them in meetings held avowedly for their benefit.

The following discussion reveals that return outmigrants (ROM) in Kerala are numerically larger in number, they have a longer history of migration, and the total human resources of this group of returnees is greater than that of their Gulf counterparts. In the over fifty year history of return of internal migrants, their cumulative contribution to the development of the state would have easily exceeded that of the Gulf returnees. Their remittances to the state are no match to the contributions of their brethren in the Gulf; but their total contribution to the development of the state would be much larger. Few the 'money orders' sent by Kerala migrants employed in the other states were used for building palatial mansions or for conspicuous consumption. Most of them were used for meeting the basic needs of the family back home: providing them better food, education and health. From the point of view of the long-term contribution of the internal migrants from Kerala, the returnees deserve as much support and recognition from the government as is planned to be given to their counterparts from the Gulf. Of course, the policies and programmes for the resettlement of returnee outmigrants would be different from those for returnee emigrants.

HISTORICAL BACKGROUND

Kerala is well known for its population migrating not only to the other states of India, but also to other countries. Historically, migration to other parts of India was the dominant trend for centuries. In recent times, migration to other countries has become the dominant feature.

Until the Second World War, Kerala was a net in-migration state. People was came to Kerala from the neighbouring states outnumbered those who moved out of Kerala. The Second World War and the independence of India changed this trend. With the demographic expansion of Kerala and the opportunities which opened up after independence, agricultural stagnation which followed agrarian reforms and the emergence of militant trade unionism in all economic sectors, youth began to move out in larger numbers to Chennai, Mumbai, Kolkota and other major cities in the country. This was purely an economic consequence of the imbalance between demographic expansion and employment opportunities in Kerala. Most of the outmigrants had all intentions of returning to Kerala once their work was over. In fact, except for those who moved into the neighbouring states of Karnataka and Tamil Nadu, most of the migrants returned once their tenure of work was over.

Some information is available about the magnitude of return internal migrants. The census, which is the major source of information on migrants in India, is not very useful in this regard. The best it can provide is the number of people who lived in other states (before the census day) but were enumerated in Kerala at the time of the census. Not only Keralites who returned to their native state are included, but also non-Keralites coming to Kerala for work or for other reasons. It is not possible to separate the two categories. It is a reasonably good assumption, however, that most of them were originally from Kerala. The numbers according to the 1971, 1981 and 1991 censuses are presented in Table 3.1. The figures show an increasing trend in the number of in-migration to Kerala: from 2,80,000 in 1971 to 3,73,000 in 1981 and further to 4,37,000 in 1991.

Most of the in-migrants in Kerala were from the neighbouring states of Tamil Nadu and Karnataka as well as from Maharashtra. These states also attracted the majority of outmigrants from Kerala. It is, therefore, reasonable to assume that in-migrants include a large number of returnees. The number of in-migrants classified by duration of residence indicates that the increase between 1981 and 1991 was only nominal, about 4,000 (2,20,000 in 1981 and 2,24,000 in 1991).

The assumption that most of the in-migrants were indeed return outmigrants is supported by the peculiar age distribution of

TABLE 3.1 PERSONS RESIDENT ELSEWHERE IN INDIA AND ENUMERATED IN KERALA CENSUSES

State of Residence Before Coming to Kerala	*Census Year*		
	1991	*1981*	*1971*
Tamil Nadu	2,72,950	2,51,064	1,94,475
Karnataka	62,172	50,034	32,225
Maharashtra	27,836	22,366	16,925
Pondicherry	15,070	9,016	6,025
Madhya Pradesh	5,960	3,995	2,600
Uttar Pradesh	5,320	3,320	3,870
Delhi	5,290	9,016	6,025
Gujarat	4,520	4,831	3,655
Total (All States)	4,37,087	3,73,127	2,79,830

Source: Zachariah, Mathew and Irudaya Rajan, 2003.

TABLE 3.2: NET MIGRATION BY AGE AND SEX, 1971-81 AND 1981-91 (SURVIVAL RATIO METHOD)

Age Group	*1981-91*	*1971-81*
0-19	+3,24,000	+4,54,000
20-39	−9,62,000	−7,54,000
40-59	−2,82,000	−3,13,000
60+	+1,78,000	+1,39,000
Total	−7,44,000	−4,74,000

Source: Zachariah, Mathew and Irudaya Rajan, 2003.

intercensal net migration. The estimates by the survival ratio method are given in Table 3.2. Although as expected total net migration was negative (outmigration exceeded in-migration), net migration at ages 60+ years was positive. In-migration (including return migration) at retirement ages (60+ years) was higher than outmigration at these ages. Many of the net gain migrants in Kerala were probably Keralites returning to their native state after their work in other states was done.

This conclusion is also substantiated by the age distribution of recent in-migrants derived from data on the duration of residence. The age distribution of in-migrants who had stayed for less than 10 years in Kerala in 1981 and 1991 is depicted in Figure 3.1. It

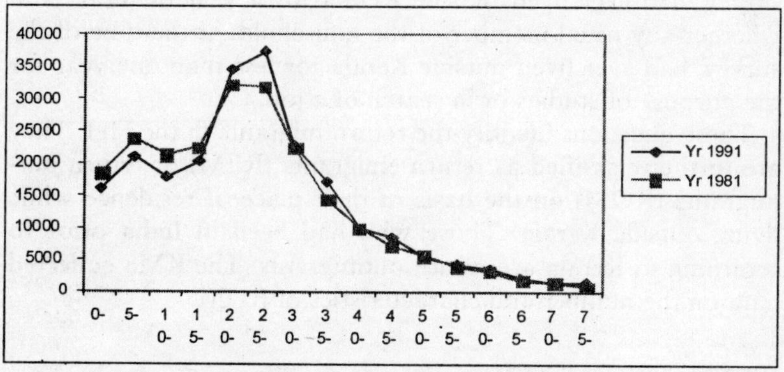

Source: Zachariah, Mathew and Irudaya Rajan, 2003.

FIGURE 3.1: AGE DISTRIBUTION OF IN-MIGRANTS TO KERALA WITH LESS THAN 10 YEARS DURATION OF STAY IN THE STATE, 1981 AND 1991

can be seen that at the prime working ages there was a real increase in the number of recent in-migrants. However, at the younger ages there was a dip and at the older ages there was no real change. As in the case of net migration estimated by the survival ratio method, these estimates also indicate a net increase in the number of migrants at the older ages. In-migrants in Kerala include a considerable number of Keralites who returned after completing their tenure of work.

The preceding discussion does not establish categorically that outmigrants of Kerala returned after working in other states. Neither does it establish the magnitude and type of outmigrants from Kerala who returned. The census data cannot answer these questions. The CDS–IDPAD Kerala Migration Study provides partial answers to some of these questions.

Return Outmigrants (ROM) from the Kerala Migration Study

The Kerala Migration Study (KMS) was based on data collected from a sample of 10,000 households selected at random from all the taluks in the state. The field work was done during March-December 1998. The heads of households were asked whether any usual member of the household (HH), at the time of the survey, had ever lived outside Kerala for a year or more; and whether any usual member of the household, at the time of the survey, had ever lived outside Kerala for less than one year for the purpose of studies or in search of a job.

These questions identify the return migrants in the HH. They are further classified as return emigrants (REM) or return outmigrants (ROM) on the basis of their place of residence while living outside Kerala. Those who had been in India prior to returning to Kerala are return outmigrants. The KMS collected data on the number and characteristics of ROM.

Return Outmigrants

In 1998, there were around 9,58,000 migrants in Kerala who had returned from other states. The same study noted that the number of return emigrants was 7,39,000. Thus, return migration

TABLE 3.3: RETURN OUTMIGRANTS AND RETURN EMIGRANTS BY DISTRICTS (IN THE ORDER OF MAGNITUDE OF ROM PER HH)

Districts	*ROM*	*REM*	*ROM/100 HH*	*REM/100 HH*
Alappuzha	1,60,481	34,572	33.6	7.2
Thrissur	1,93,238	1,16,788	30.7	18.6
Palakkad	1,17,891	39,238	22.1	7.4
Pathanamthitta	52,034	54,537	17.7	18.5
Kollam	83,759	74,106	15.0	13.2
Trivandrum	95,709	1,18,878	14.6	18.1
Wayanad	20,436	3,327	13.0	2.1
Kottayam	49,220	18,164	12.6	4.6
Kasaragod	22,198	16,667	11.0	8.2
Kozhikode	50,211	60,910	9.5	11.5
Ernakulam	45,272	45,028	7.4	7.4
Kannur	34,176	28,263	7.4	6.1
Malappuram	26,655	1,23,750	4.4	20.5
Idukki	7,546	5,017	3.0	2.0
Kerala	9,58,826	7,39,245	15.1	11.6

Source: Zachariah, Mathew and Irudaya Rajan, 2003.

from within the country exceeded return migration from outside India by a wide margin (Table 3.3). Similarly, the number of return outmigrants exceeded the number of outmigrants (6,91,000) who were living outside the state at the time of the survey.

For every 100 households in the state there were 15 return outmigrants compared to only 12 return emigrants or 11 outmigrants. Thus, migrants who returned to Kerala after living elsewhere in the country comprised an important segment of the population of the state, for more important than the more vocal group of migrants who returned from abroad.

REGIONAL ASPECT: DISTRICTS

The highest number of ROM was in Thrissur district, i.e. 1,93,000 or one-fifth of the total. The least number was in Idukki district, i.e. 7,500 return outmigrants or less than 1 per cent of the total. While in the state as a whole, every 100 households had nearly 15 ROM; in Alappuzha district the ratio was 34:100. Out of the fourteen districts in the state only four (Alappuzha, Thrissur, Palakkad and Pathanamthitta) had more ROM per 100 HHs than the state average. The southern districts in general had more ROM than the northern districts. Idukki, a new district, was an exception with fewer ROM in absolute or relative terms.

Origin of Return Outmigrants

The largest number of return outmigrants in Kerala came from Maharashtra, particularly Mumbai. This was followed by Tamil Nadu and Karnataka. Though there was an overall association between the number of return migrants and the number of outmigrants, the association was not perfect. More migrants in the neighbouring states tended to stay back than those in the far-fuing states. A greater number of migrants in Mumbai wanted to come back than those who were in Chennai or Bangalore (Table 3.4).

TABLE 3.4: DISTRIBUTION OF RETURN OUTMIGRANTS BY STATE OF ORIGIN

State of Origin	*% of Total ROM*
Maharashtra	26.5
Tamil Nadu	25.9
Karnataka	14.2
Delhi	4.5
Andhra Pradesh	3.6
Gujarat	3.2
Madhya Pradesh	2.6
Punjab	2.5
Uttar Pradesh	1.8
Orissa	1.4
West Bengal	1.2
Assam	1.1
Rajasthan	0.9
Bihar	0.5
Pondicherry	0.2
Other States	9.9
Total	100.0

Source: Zachariah, Mathew and Irudaya Rajan, 2003.

TREND IN RETURN OUTMIGRATION

The trend in the return of outmigrants during the 1980-98 period is presented in Table 3.5 and Figure 3.2. It should be borne in mind that these figures represent survivors of ROM after attrition through death and further outmigration or emigration. The figure for a particular year is net return outmigrants after allowing for these factors. As a result, increases in the numbers are over-estimated.

The increases were small during the earlier periods, but in recent years there has been a spurt in return of outmigrants. Return of outmigrants has decreased compared to return of emigrants in recent years. The gap is likely to widen in future. Overall, an increasing trend was seen in the number of return

TABLE 3.5: TREND IN ROM AND REM, 1980-98

	ROM	*REM*
Before 1980	1,65,360	28,667
1980	28,105	3,050
1981	20,915	3,050
1982	20,261	7,319
1983	28,758	15,248
1984	20,261	7,319
1985	28,105	16,468
1986	29,412	19,518
1987	18,954	10,978
1988	46,405	28,667
1989	30,065	17,688
1990	41,830	37,206
1991	30719	20,128
1992	42484	43,306
1993	44,445	35,376
1994	56,863	57,944
1995	64,052	73,193
1996	75,164	1,07,959
1997	88,236	1,27,477
1998*	78,432	78,682

Note: * For part of 1998 only.
Source: Zachariah, Mathew and Irudaya Rajan, 2003.

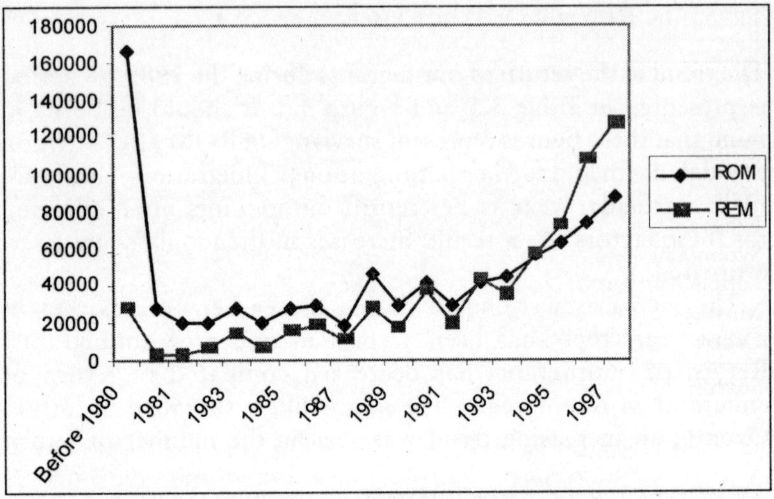

Source: Zachariah, Mathew and Irudaya Rajan, 2003.

FIGURE 3.2: TREND IN ROM AND REM, 1980-97

outmigrants. The increase assumed considerable strength after 1993. Since 1993, the number of ROM exceeded the number of REM, but in more recent years return emigrants outnumbered return outmigrants.

Return Outmigrants by Community

The highest number of return outmigrants belonged to the Nair and Ezhava communities (20 per cent each). The lowest number was from the Scheduled Castes and Muslim communities. There were few ROM among Christians than among the major Hindu communities. If we take into account the overall size of the communities, a different picture emerges. Syrian Christians topped the list when we considered ROM per household. Nairs were not far behind. Muslims, who were ahead of all other communities with respect to REM, were at the bottom in the case of ROM. Outmigration and return outmigration were predominant among Syrian Christians and Nairs (Table 3.6).

TABLE 3.6: ROM BY COMMUNITY, PER CENT DISTRIBUTION AND RATE PER 100 HOUSEHOLDS

	%		*Per 100 HS*	
	ROM	*REM*	*ROM*	*REM*
SC/ST	7.4	1.7	10.3	2.3
Nair	20.9	7.0	18.1	7.1
Ezhava	20.4	19.1	12.8	10.7
Syrian Christian	14.0	10.4	19.2	12.3
Latin Christian	12.7	10.5	10.2	12.7
Muslim	8.7	45.3	5.7	25.4
Others	16.0	6.0	18.7	6.5

Source: Zachariah, Mathew and Irudaya Rajan, 2003.

CHARACTERISTICS OF RETURN OUTMIGRANTS

Demographic Characteristics

There were fewer females among return outmigrants compared to the general population, but a higher proportion than among return emigrants. Females constituted 29 per cent of ROM compared to 51 per cent among the general population and 11 per cent among REM (Table 3.7).

TABLE 3.7: PROPORTION OF FEMALES AMONG RETURN OUTMIGRANTS

Trivandrum	37.2
Kollam	18.5
Pathanamthitta	23.0
Alappuzha	45.3
Kottayam	8.8
Idukki	36.4
Ernakulam	32.9
Thrissur	24.1
Palakkad	40.4
Malappuram	7.9
Kozhikode	15.8
Wayanad	32.4
Kannur	13.6
Kasaragod	33.3
Kerala	29.2

Source: Zachariah, Mathew and Irudaya Rajan, 2003.

TABLE 3.8: PROPORTION OF FEMALES BY COMMUNITY, REM AND ROM

	ROM	*REM*	*Total*
SC/ST	27.7	14.3	51.8
Nair	26.9	18.1	52.6
Ezhava	23.4	12.7	51.8
Syrian Christian	27.8	24.6	51.3
Latin Christian	34.3	8.4	51.5
Muslim	17.4	7.6	52.3
Others	40.4	1.4	51.3
All Communities	29.2	10.9	52.0

Source: Zachariah, Mathew and Irudaya Rajan, 2003.

The proportion of females among return outmigrants varied considerably by the district of origin. On the whole, the proportion was higher among the southern districts; it was highest in Alappuzha and lowest in Malappuram districts. The number of females among return outmigrants varied considerably by community also. Latin Christian ROM included the highest proportion of females and Muslims the least (Table 3.8).

Age Composition

It is generally expected that return outmigrants are old people who return to their native state after completing their tenure of work outside Kerala. However, this study demonstrated that this was not true; many ROM were young. Nearly 25 per cent of ROM were in the age group of 15-29 years and 36 per cent were in the 30-44 years age group. The proportion of older persons (60+ years) among ROM was only slightly higher (around one-eighth) than the corresponding proportion in the general population (Table 3.9).

While the average age of return outmigrants did not vary greatly from that of the general population or return emigrants, the proportions of migrants in the younger age groups were very much different (see Figure 3.3). For example, in the 15-24 years are group, the figures were 25 per cent for ROM, 8 per cent for REM and 34 per cent among the general population. Significant variations were also observed in the age composition of ROM by community.

TABLE 3.9: AGE DISTRIBUTION OF ROM BY COMMUNITY

Age (Years)	*Nair*	*Ezhava*	*Syrian Christian*	*Latin Christian*	*Muslim*	*All Communities*
0-14	3.8	3.6	8.0	15.2	3.3	6.2
15-29	20.2	29.9	22.6	22.8	30.6	25.1
30-44	35.7	39.4	32.2	42.4	29.8	36.3
45-59	25.1	16.8	23.6	13.3	22.3	19.9
60+	15.2	10.2	13.6	6.3	14.0	12.4
Total	100.0	100.0	100.0	100.0	100.0	100.0

Source: Zachariah, Mathew and Irudaya Rajan, 2003.

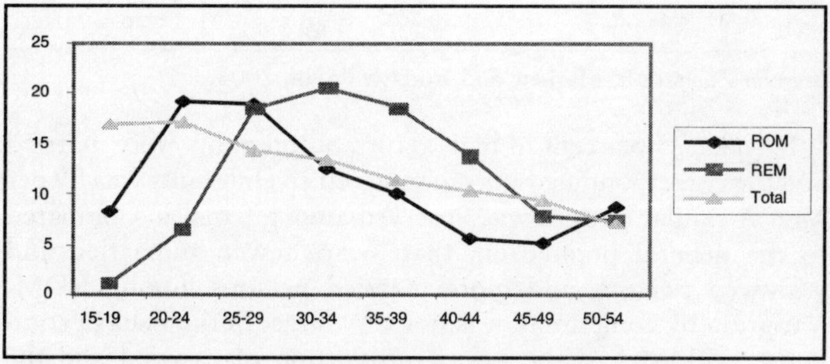

Source: Zachariah, Mathew and Irudaya Rajan, 2003.

FIGURE 3.3: AGE DISTRIBUTION OF MIGRANTS AND THE TOTAL POPULATION

The proportion of persons in the 15-29 years age group was highest among Muslims and Ezhavas and lowest among Syrian Christians. The proportion in the 30-44 years age group was highest among Latin Christians and lowest among Nairs. The number of persons in the 45-59 years age group was highest among Nairs and lowest among Latin Christians. In the 60+ age group, Nairs accounted for 15.2 per cent compared to 6.3 per cent among Latin Christians. On the whole, ROM in the Nair community were older than those in all other communities. They were followed by Muslims, Syrian Christians, Ezhavas and Latin Christians, in that order.

Marital Status Distribution

As expected, three-fourths of ROM were married. Around one-fifth were unmarried. Widowhood ratio was 3.6 per cent. There were very few widowed or separated among return outmigrants (Table 3.10).

TABLE 3.10: PROPORTION MARRIED BY MIGRATION STATUS

	% Married	
	Males	*Females*
ROM	75.1	75.1
OMI	18.8	49.1
REM	89.2	77.8
EMI	49.8	79.2

Source: Zachariah, Mathew and Irudaya Rajan, 2003.

Further, 75 per cent of male return outmigrants were married and the corresponding figure among return emigrants was 89 per cent. A similar pattern was observed among females. Compared to the general population, there were fewer unmarried and widowed persons and more married persons among ROM. Variation by community was not very large. In the Ezhava community, ROM had the lowest proportion of married and the highest proportion of unmarried persons. The highest proportion of married persons was in the Nair and Muslim communities. Widowhood rate was highest among ROM in the Nair community and lowest among ROM in the Muslim community (Table 3.11).

Socio-economic Characteristics

Education: In general, internal migrants were better educated than external migrants. Among the various migrant groups, outmigrants were the most educated (Table 3.12). It is possible that some internal migrants returned home as they had failed to get a job because of their relatively low educational levels.

The number of degree holders was 13 per cent among return outmigrants compared to 5 per cent in the general population. Similarly, the number of persons with secondary level education

TABLE 3.11: MARITAL STATUS DISTRIBUTION BY COMMUNITY

	All	Community					
	Population	*ROM*	*N*	*E*	*Sy*	*La*	*M*
Single	28.0	20.7	15.6	26.9	20.1	22.5	21.2
Married	62.7	75.1	78.6	70.1	76.1	76.1	78.0
Widowed	8.1	3.6	5.3	2.7	3.3	0.7	0.8
Divorced	0.5	0.1	0.4	0.4	0.5	0.7	0.0
Separated	0.7	0.5	0.0	0.0	0.0	0.0	0.0
Total	100.0	100.0	100.0	100.0	100.0	100.0	100.0

Notes: N = Nair, E = Ezhava; Sy = Syrian Christian; La = Latin Christian; M = Muslims.
Source: Zachariah, Mathew and Irudaya Rajan, 2003.

TABLE 3.12: PER CENT WITH SECONDARY LEVEL OF EDUCATION

	Secondary or a Degree Level Education
OMI	60.6
ROM	42.7
EMI	40.5
REM	30.9

Source: Zachariah, Mathew and Irudaya Rajan, 2003.

was 30 per cent among return outmigrants as opposed to 19 per cent in the general population.

There were vast inter-community differences among return outmigrants. ROM in the Nair and Syrian Christian communities were better educated, 60 per cent of them had completed SSLC or had a degree. Among Muslims, ROM were the least educated, as only 15 per cent of them had secondary or higher levels of education. Ezhavas and Latin Christians fell in between, but their educational level was lower than the average level for all ROM taken together (Table 3.13).

A comparison of the educational level of outmigrants and return outmigrants revealed that education was an important determinant of internal migration and that the degree of success of outmigrants was partly determined by their educational levels.

TABLE 3.13: DISTRIBUTION BY EDUCATIONAL ATTAINMENT, .RETURN OUTMIGRANTS BY COMMUNITY

	Community						
	N	*E*	*Sy*	*La*	*M*	*ROM*	*POP*
Below Primary	2.2	7.0	3.0	6.0	20.7	9.4	21.1
Primary	10.1	14.3	10.6	19.9	28.1	14.7	20.5
Below Secondary	27.6	40.7	26.3	37.3	36.4	33.1	34.8
Secondary	40.7	27.8	42.9	28.3	11.6	29.5	18.6
Degree	19.4	10.3	17.2	8.4	3.3	13.2	5.0
Total	100.0	100.0	100.0	100.0	100.0	100.0	100.0
% Secondary + Degree	60.1	38.1	60.1	36.7	14.9	42.7	23.6

Notes: N = Nair; E = Ezhava; Sy = Syrian Christian; La = Latin Christian; M = Muslim.

Source: Zachariah, Mathew and Irudaya Rajan, 2003.

OCCUPATION

The age distribution of return outmigrants indicated that not all of them were retired. This was substantiated by their current occupational composition. About 74 per cent of them were engaged in different types of productive employment, as against 72 per cent in the general population in the case of males; and 19 per cent compared with 17 per cent among females in the general population. However, a higher proportion of male ROM were job seekers. The proportion of retired and superannuated was higher among ROM (Table 3.14).

A relatively higher number of ROM was employed in government and semi-government jobs: 10 per cent males (compared to 5 per cent in the general population) and 4 per cent females (as opposed to 2 per cent in the general population). The differentials in the occupational composition by community are presented in Table 3.15.

These were large differentials in several occupational categories. The percentage of persons in government employment varied from 11.5 among Nairs to 0.8 among Muslims. In the self-employment category, the percentages varied from 23.7 among Muslims to 15.3 among Nairs. Large differentials were noted in

TABLE 3.14: OCCUPATION OF TOTAL POPULATION (POP) AND RETURN OUTMIGRANTS (ROM) BY SEX

	Males		*Females*	
	Pop	*Rom*	*Pop*	*Rom*
Government Employment	5.2	9.9	1.9	4.3
Employee of Semi-government	1.4	1.7	0.8	1.5
Private Sector Employee	6.2	7.1	2.1	1.8
Self-employed	23.3	23.9	3.8	6.1
Unpaid Worker	1.7	0.9	0.6	0.3
Agricultural Labour	8.1	6.1	3.5	2.6
Non-agricultural Labour	26.5	24.4	4.2	2.0
Job Seekers	5.8	6.1	5.1	9.9
Job not Required	9.6	14.9	7.5	5.6
Student	10.4	3.5	9.2	6.9
Domestic Work	0.7	0.3	60.9	58.4
Pensioners/Elderly	0.9	1.2	0.4	0.5
Total	100.0	100.0	100.0	100.0

Source: Zachariah, Mathew and Irudaya Rajan, 2003.

TABLE 3.15: PER CENT OF RETURN OUTMIGRANTS IN SELECTED OCCUPATIONS BY COMMUNITY

	Nairs	*Ezhavas*	*Syrian Christians*	*Latin Christians*	*Muslims*
State/Central Government	11.5	8.7	7.1	5.6	0.8
Private Sector	5.7	5.7	9.3	6.3	4.2
Self-employment	15.3	17.8	23.0	20.4	23.7
Agricultural Labour	3.4	5.3	1.6	4.2	3.4
Non-agricultural Labour	8.0	26.1	7.7	21.1	28.8
Unemployed	9.9	8.3	6.6	3.5	5.1
Not in LF	42.0	26.5	42.0	38.0	33.1

Source: Zachariah, Mathew and Irudaya Rajan, 2003.

the non-agricultural labour category, 29 per cent among Muslims compared to 8 per cent among Syrian Christians.

Defining the first three occupational categories as higher status occupations, it was noted that Syrian Christians were far ahead of other communities with respect to higher status occupations.

Nairs, Ezhavas and Latin Christians were at the same level. Muslims accounted for the smallest proportion in the higher status occupations.

HOUSING AND HOUSEHOLD AMENITIES

Value of House

In general, return outmigrants had relatively modest houses compared to those of other categories of migrants. However, they had better housing compared to non-migrants (Table 3.16).

TABLE 3.16: INDEX OF THE VALUE OF HOUSE BY MIGRATION STATUS

Return Outmigrant	486
Return Emigrant	644
Outmigrant	502
Emigrant	705
Non-migrant	430

Source: Zachariah, Mathew and Irudaya Rajan, 2003.

A slightly different picture emerged when the distribution of households by quality of the house was compared. The number of 'luxurious', 'very good' and 'good' houses was higher among return outmigrants than among non-migrants. However, their houses were of lower quality compared to those of international migrants (Table 3.17).

Among the major communities in Kerala, the quality of housing of Syrian Christians was the best. Almost 24 per cent of their

TABLE 3.17: DISTRIBUTION OF HOUSES BY QUALITY

	ROM HHs	*Non-migrant HHs*
Luxurious	1.3	1.0
Very Good	14.5	9.6
Good	60.5	54.3
Poor	13.9	21.9
Kutcha	9.7	13.3
Total	100.0	100.0

Source: Zachariah, Mathew and Irudaya Rajan, 2003.

TABLE 3.18: QUALITY OF HOUSES BY COMMUNITY

Quality	*All*	*Nair*	*Ezhava*	*Syrian Christian*	*Latin Christian*	*Muslim*
Luxurious	1.1	2.6	0.4	1.0	0.0	0.8
Very Good	17.1	20.0	12.0	22.6	21.1	16.5
Good	61.4	65.9	63.1	69.3	55.4	63.6
Poor	11.8	8.1	14.2	5.0	16.9	9.9
Kutcha	8.6	3.3	10.2	2.0	6.6	9.1
Total	100.0	100.0	100.0	100.0	100.0	100.0
Per cent Luxurious + Very Good	18.2	22.6	12.4	23.6	21.1	17.4

Source: Zachariah, Mathew and Irudaya Rajan, 2003.

houses were either luxurious or very good. Nairs and Muslims were not far behind. The houses of Ezhavas were of low quality and almost one-fourth of their houses were either poor or kutcha (Table 3.18).

HOUSING AMENITIES

ELECTRIFICATION

In 1998, nearly three-fourths of the houses in Kerala were electrified. Among the households of ROM, 81 per cent had electrification. The figures were higher for all types of migrants' households compared to those of non-migrant households (Table 3.19).

TABLE 3.19: PER CENT OF HOUSES ELECTRIFIED BY MIGRATION STATUS

Migrant Group	*% Houses Electrified*
Return Outmigrant	81.2
Return Emigrant	87.4
Outmigrant	83.4
Emigrant	89.6
Non-migrant	66.4
All	73.6

Source: Zachariah, Mathew and Irudaya Rajan, 2003.

TABLE 3.20: PER CENT OF HOUSES ELECTRIFIED BY COMMUNITY, ROM

	% Electrified Houses of Return Outmigrants
SC/ST	60.0
Nair	89.5
Ezhava	75.0
Syrian Christian	92.1
Latin Christian	78.9
Muslim	73.5
Others	85.2
All	81.2

Source: Zachariah, Mathew and Irudaya Rajan, 2003.

As in the case of quality of housing, Syrian Christians were ahead of all other communities with respect to the percentage of houses electrified. Muslims were at the bottom (Table 3.20).

COOKING FUEL

The use of fuel for cooking is a good index of the socio-economic status of a population. In this respect, return outmigrants compared well with outmigrants or non-migrants. However, they lagged behind external migrants (Table 3.21).

Inter-community comparison of the proportion of households using LP gas throws no new light on the relative socio-economic status of the various communities. Syrian Christians were ahead

TABLE 3.21: PER CENT HOUSEHOLDS USING LP GAS FOR COOKING

Migrant Group	*% Houses using LPG for Cooking*
Return Outmigrant	27.1
Return Emigrant	30.2
Outmigrant	25.8
Emigrant	30.2
Non-migrant	13.5
All	19.0

Source: Zachariah, Mathew and Irudaya Rajan, 2003.

TABLE 3.22: PER CENT HOUSEHOLDS USING LP GAS FOR COOKING BY COMMUNITY

	% Houses using LPG for Cooking Among Return Outmigrants
SC/ST	7.7
Nair	33.8
Ezhava	17.1
Syrian Christian	49.3
Latin Christian	28.4
Muslim	22.4
Others	22.4
All	27.1

Source: Zachariah, Mathew and Irudaya Rajan, 2003.

of all others. Nearly half the households of return outmigrants of the Syrian Christian community used LP gas compared to 17 per cent among those of the Ezhava community (Table 3.22).

Possession of Household Consumer Durables

Migration and the consequent increase in disposable income is a major factor determining the number and variety of consumer durables in households. Kerala is often used as a test market by many companies producing these goods.

Internal migration had a lesser effect on the acquisition of consumer durables than external migration. The possession of common household goods (including crockery, furniture and other consumer durables) classified in terms of the migration status of the household is given in Table 3.24. An index based on these percentages is given in Table 3.23. The index is 27 for return

TABLE 3.23: INDEX OF POSSESSION OF HOUSEHOLD GOODS BY MIGRATION STATUS

Type of Household	*Index*
1. Return Outmigrant	27
2. Outmigrant	22
3. Return Emigrant	32
4. Emigrant	32
5. Non-migrant	15

Source: Zachariah, Mathew and Irudaya Rajan, 2003.

TABLE 3.24: PER CENT OF HOUSEHOLDS POSSESSING SELECTED CONSUMER DURABLES

Consumer Durables	*ROM*	*Non-migrant*
Motor Car	5	2
Motorcycle	18	8
Telephone	22	11
Television	53	34
VCR	14	6
Water Pump	35	22
Sewing Machine	25	14
Refrigerator	33	13
Fan	72	47
Gas Stove	37	15
Clock	87	76
Iron	61	37

Source: Zachariah, Mathew and Irudaya Rajan, 2003.

outmigrant households compared to 32 for external migrants and 15 for households with no migrants.

A comparison of the use of individual consumer items revealed that a higher proportion of return outmigrant households possessed television, refrigerator, gas stove, etc., than non-migrant households. Undoubtedly, migration is a means of acquiring modern household consumer durables (Table 3.24).

RETURN OUTMIGRANTS AND OTHER MIGRANT GROUPS

Return Outmigrants and Return Emigrants

As mentioned in the introduction, one of the objectives here is to argue that return outmigrants deserve as much support from the government is as provided to return emigrants. In terms of current numbers, return outmigrants outnumbered return emigrants by 39 per cent. It is certain that their numerical superiority will continue for a long time to come.

The proportion of men among return outmigrants was lower than among return emigrants. Besides, fewer persons were in the prime working age group of 20-49 years and a higher percentage was unmarried. Educationwise, they were far superior to return

TABLE 3.25: SOCIO-ECONOMIC CHARACTERISTICS OF RETURN OUTMIGRANTS AND RETURN EMIGRANTS

		ROM %	*REM*
Proportion of Males		70.9	88.9
Proportion in the 20-49 Years Age Group		71.2	85.5
Proportion Married:	Males	75.1	89.2
	Females	75.1	77.8
Proportion with Secondary Certificate or Degree		42.7	30.9
Proportion in Higher Status Occupation		34.0	45.8
Proportion with 'Very Good' House		15.9	24.4
Proportion with Electric Connection		81.2	87.4
Proportion with LPG Supply		27.1	30.2
Index of Possession of Consumer Durables		27.0	32.0

Source: Zachariah, Mathew and Irudaya Rajan, 2003.

emigrants; 31 per cent of return emigrants had completed SSLC or had higher qualifications, whereas the corresponding figure for return outmigrants was 42 per cent. However, they included fewer persons in high status occupations. Regarding the quality of housing, return outmigrants were a notch lower than return emigrants. Thus, return outmigrants were superior to return emigrants only in terms of educational achievement (Table 3.25).

Return Outmigrants and Outmigrants

All return outmigrants had been naturally outmigrants. As can be seen from Table 3.26, around 75 per cent of return outmigrants were married and only 19 per cent of outmigrants were married. When they left the state, they were largely unmarried, but when they returned most of them were married at the time of outmigration. A large number got married after outmigration. The differentials in marital status distribution were more marked in the case of males than females.

While 61 per cent of outmigrants had completed SSLC or had higher educational qualifications, the corresponding percentage for return outmigrants was 43. Two factors may explain this differential. First, those who returned were probably 'failures' among outmigrants. Those with lower educational qualifications could not compete for good jobs and, therefore, decided to return.

TABLE 3.26: SOCIO-ECONOMIC CHARACTERISTICS OF RETURN OUTMIGRANTS AND OUTMIGRANTS

	ROM	*OMI*
Proportion of Males	70.9	75.9
Proportion in the 20-49 Years Age Group	71.2	70.5
Proportion Married: Males	75.1	18.8
Females	75.1	49.2
Proportion with Secondary Certificate or Degree	42.7	60.6
Proportion in Higher Status Occupation	34.0	45.8
Proportion with 'Very Good' or Better House	15.9	13.9
Proportion with Electric Connection	81.2	83.4
Proportion with LPG Supply	27.1	25.8
Index of Possession of Consumer Durables	27.0	22.0

Source: Zachariah, Mathew and Irudaya Rajan, 2003.

Second, was the trend effect. Return outmigrants, belonged to an earlier cohort whose educational level was in general lower. Outmigrants, on the other hand, belonged to more recent cohorts whose average educational level was much higher. The differentials in occupation may be a reflection of the differentials in educational level.

Return Outmigrants and Emigrants

The differentials in socio-economic factors were highest between return outmigrants and emigrants. Return outmigrants fared better than emigrants in the area of educational attainment (Table 3.27).

Return Outmigrants and Non-migrants

Return outmigrants compared favourably with non-migrants with respect to all socio-economic indices. Return outmigrants included a higher percentage of males, persons in the prime working age groups and married persons (Table 3.28). The differentials in terms of education and occupation were also large. ROM had better housing, more facilities at home and possessed more consumer durables. In every respect, return outmigrants fared better than those who did not migrate at all either to the other states in India or to other countries.

TABLE 3.27: SOCIO-ECONOMIC CHARACTERISTICS OF RETURN OUTMIGRANTS AND EMIGRANTS

	ROM	*EMI*
Proportion of Males	70.9	90.7
Proportion in the 20-49 Years Age Group	71.2	90.8
Proportion Married: Males	75.1	89.2
Females	75.1	77.8
Proportion with Secondary Certificate or Degree	42.7	40.5
Proportion in Higher Status Occupation	34.0	45.8
Proportion with 'Very Good' or 'Better' house	15.9	24.9
Proportion with Electric Connection	81.2	89.6
Proportion with LPG Supply	27.1	30.2
Index of Possession of Consumer Durables	27.0	32.0

Source: Zachariah, Mathew and Irudaya Rajan, 2003.

TABLE 3.28: SOCIO-ECONOMIC CHARACTERISTICS OF RETURN OUTMIGRANTS AND NON-MIGRANTS

	ROM	*NMI*
Proportion of Males	70.9	50.1
Proportion in the 20-49 Years Age Group	71.2	36.1
Proportion Married: Males	75.1	61.9
Females	75.1	60.6
Proportion with Secondary Certificate or Degree	42.7	22.0
Proportion in Higher Status Occupation	34.0	9.3
Proportion with 'Very Good' or Better House	15.9	10.6
Proportion with Electric Connection	81.2	66.4
Proportion with LPG Supply	27.1	13.5
Index of Possession of Consumer Durables	27.0	15.0

Source: Zachariah, Mathew and Irudaya Rajan, 2003.

DETERMINANTS OF RETURN OUTMIGRATION

To some extent determinants of return outmigration should be related to determinants of outmigration. Outmigration is a necessary but not sufficient condition for return migration, as there is no requirement that all outmigrants should return. In fact, many of them do not return. Specific factors are associated with return migration.

The motivation for outmigration from Kerala as in most other parts of the world is predominantly economic. People migrate from Kerala to other places in India in search of better opportunities for employment and income and for raising resources necessary for improving their standard of living on a sustainable basis.

To the extent that high unemployment and low wages (in the earlier decades) are partly a result of high population density and high population growth rates, demographic factors may be perceived as a major cause of outmigration. But demography is not the only factor involved in outmigration. The failure of local institutions to provide the needed support and to create a milieu conducive to economic growth seems to be an equally important factor.

Although demographic pressure continues to be very high in Kerala (it has among the highest population densities in India), the likelihood of its increase in the coming decades is drastically reduced. Fertility rates have remained below replacement level in recent years and emigration has contributed to a reduction in unemployment. Unlike in the past, wage rates are no longer low; indeed, they are among the highest in India. Emigration to the Gulf countries has opened up an alternative to migration to the other states of India. There are a number of other factors which determine the rate of return outmigration, besides the necessary condition of outmigration itself.

In the past, cost of living was relatively low in Kerala. Today, it is among the highest for any state in the country. Outmigrants who are accustomed to low costs of living in their destination of migration are normally hesitant to return to Kerala for fear of the high costs of living there.

Education is an important factor not only influencing outmigration, but also determining the chances of rehabilitation on return. As noted earlier, the educational levels of return outmigrants were lower than those of outmigrants. The inability to secure a good job because of poor educational qualifications could be one of the factors influencing their decision to return to Kerala.

In the past, the bulk of outmigrants from Kerala comprised workers or prospective workers and not their entire families. Today, families join the migrants at their places of work more often than in the past. Migrants accompanied by their families are less likely to return than migrants who have left their families back home. Thus, there is not as much compulsion for most migrants to return home as it was in the past. A higher number of Kerala migrants settle down in their places of work outside the state rather than return home where the cost of living is higher and life conditions more difficult.

Low birth rate, high levels of school and college enrolment and large-scale emigration of skilled and unskilled persons to the Gulf countries have made the supply of artisans, craftsmen and other skilled workers scarce in Kerala's job market. It has become easier to hire a graduate engineer than to recruit a housemaid for domestic work or a person to look after the increasing number of the elderly in the state. Skilled workers like carpenters and plumbers are far more scarce than engineers or doctors. Life for the retired has become difficult and expensive in Kerala. This is a major factor influencing migrants' decision whether to return to Kerala or to continue to live in their place of work outside Kerala.

A new phenomenon affecting the return of outmigrants is the opening up of the Gulf countries to emigrants from Kerala. Some of the outmigrants availed of this opportunity and found work in the Gulf countries. When they returned they were no longer return outmigrants but return emigrants. Gulf migration has tended to reduce the number of return outmigrants.

For some outmigrants who did not want to return to Kerala for one reason or another, several 'better' choices were available. For many well-to-do migrants, Bangalore, Chennai, Ooty or Kodaiknal were better places to settle down than any place in Kerala. Political demonstrations, hartals and worker strikes, which are a regular phenomena in several parts of the state, and the practice of 'attimary' as well as other acts of labour militancy deter many prospective return outmigrants from settling down in Kerala and compel them to choose other destinations for their permanent residence.

Future Trend and Pattern of Kerala's Return Outmigration

What is the implication of these determinants for the future trend in return outmigration to Kerala? Will it increase or decrease?

There are a number of reasons why the number of return outmigrants should increase. The large number of outmigrants living outside the state is an important factor in this respect.

The recent demographic trend in Kerala is another important factor. The average family size is less than 2 children per couple. It has been below replacement level for more than a decade now. In the coming decades, the population at the younger ages is expected to decline further. According to one projection, the number of persons in the 20-34 years age group is expected to decline from about 8.66 million in 2001 to 5.07 million in 2051. Similarly, the number of persons in the 35-49 years age group is expected to increase till 2011 and then decrease from 8.46 million in 2011 to 6.07 million in 2051 (see Figure 3.4).

In the long run, these demographic changes may play a significant role in determining the magnitude of return outmigrants in Kerala. Due to the implications of such changes for the labour force, they are likely to act as a positive inducement for the pravasi Malayalees to return home. On the other hand, the adverse political climate, labour militancy and stagnancy in the productive sectors of the economy are likely to deter outmigrants from returning to Kerala.

On the whole, however, it is unlikely that in the near future there would be any major change in the volume of return

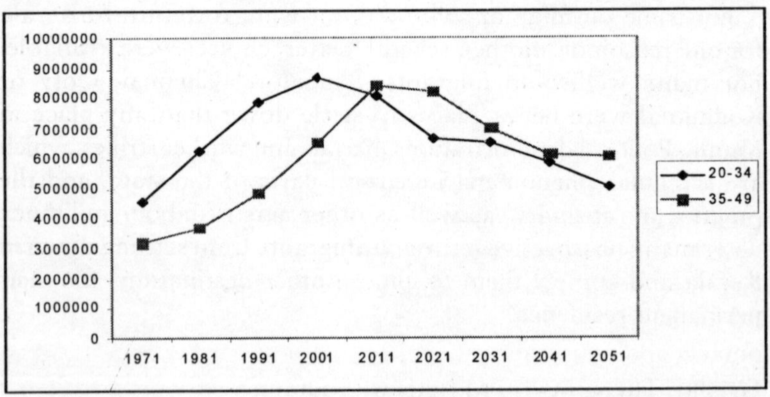

Source: Irudaya Rajan and Zachariah, 1998.

FIGURE 3.4: POPULATION GROWTH IN YOUNG WORKING AGES, 20-34 YEARS AND 35-49 YEARS, KERALA, 1971-2051

outmigrants in Kerala. There would be some decline in the number of return outmigrants in the short run.

Policy Considerations

The following policy recommendations are based on a few premises.

First, in the changed demographic scenario, in which the number of young working people is expected to significantly decline in absolute terms, it is in the interest of the state to encourage outmigrants to return from other states.

Second, a new phenomenon is Kerala is the in-migration of workers, especially manual workers, in significant numbers from other states. These workers are employed in such sectors as building construction and road construction. Often they are paid lower wages than the prevailing rates for local workers. The net outcome is rising unemployment among local workers and a decline in the prevailing wage rates. In future, with a further decline in the young population, in-migration of workers from outside the state is likely to accelerate. This new trend calls for a close examination through special studies.

Third, since outmigrants are more educated than the general population of the state, their return could contribute significantly to improving the human resources base of the state.

Fourth, Kerala's location at the southern most tip of the Indian subcontinent, far from the heartland of the country, makes it possible for the well-experienced return outmigrants to contribute substantially to the integration of the state with rest of the country.

Fifth, in view of the prevailing economic and employment scenario, migration, internal or external, is one of the best options available to the youth for upward socio-economic mobility. Therefore, while the state should continue to promote emigration and outmigration, it should also encourage migrants' continued contacts and relationship with the community back home.

What policies and programmes should the state undertake to attract migrants to return home? Migrants living in the other states of India believe that their interests are brushed aside compared to those of migrants living abroad. The government should make efforts to allay this apprehension. Many of the problems of internal migrants are similar to those of external migrants.

External migrants demand government's assistance in introducing more flights and reducing air fare to and from the Gulf countries. Internal migrants want more frequent and convenient railway connections to different destinations within the country. Financial assistance for the construction of houses during their sojourn outside Kerala would be a major incentive for migrants to return.

Special quotas are reserved for external migrants in the admissions to colleges and technical institutions. Why not extend similar facilities to the Malayalis living in other states within India? It is not only with respect to college admissions, but also in many other areas where the Gulf Malayalis are pampered. The government should make a conscious effort to avoid discrimination between internal and international migrants.

On the basis of this discussion, some policy recommendations are in order.

1. In the changed demographic scenario, return migration should be welcomed by the state. The government should provide incentives to encourage them to return to Kerala instead of continuing to stay in their places of work or settling down in Bangalore, Chennai or other mellow destinations.
2. The government should not discriminate between external and internal migrants in terms of policies and programmes for migrants.
3. NORKA or a similar organization should be set up to look after the interests of internal migrants.
4. Kerala needs an organization, preferably outside the government, to monitor migration from the state, return migration to the state and the newly developing and sustained in-migration of manual workers from other states. The MMC (Migration Monitoring Centre) should collect and disseminate statistical and analytical data on out-migration and emigration and return emigration and

return outmigration as well as on in-migration and its return. It should advice the state on migration policies and programmes. In addition to Gulf migration, the emerging in-migration of workers from other states and its impact on unemployment levels and wage rates in Kerala call for special studies, a task which may be under taken by the proposed MMC.

CHAPTER 4

The Changing Profile of Return Emigrants

The profile of migration in all its different phases has undergone changes over time. This chapter presents an overview of the changes in the composition of return emigrants (*a*) at the pre-emigration phase, namely, their spatial distribution; age, sex and educational qualifications; and emigration costs; (*b*) at the expatriate phase in terms of destination of emigration, working and living conditions in the destination countries; and (*c*) the post-return phase such as the conditions of emigrants at home in terms of economic and occupational status. This overview is based primarily on a comparison between an earlier study of return emigrants in 1985 (Nair, 1991) and the present study.

A. THE PRE-EMIGRATION PHASE

The spatial distribution of emigrants has not undergone any significant change during the past two decades (Table 4.1). In terms of absolute numbers emigration increased by nearly 6.5 times during the two decades since 1980. Around 18 per cent of emigrants were non-working dependents in 1998.

The Malabar area comprising the districts of Kasargode, Kannur, Wayanad, Kozhikode and Malappuram accounted for nearly 45 per cent of the total emigrant population to the Middle East in both years. In the central districts of Kerala, i.e. Ernakulam and Trichur, the proportion declined from 22 per cent to 16 per cent. Correspondingly, the proportionate importance of the southern districts (Idukki, Kottayam, Alleppey, Pathanamthitta, Kollam and Thiruvananthapuram) increased from less than one-third to almost 40 per cent. The relative importance of Trichur district declined drastically from nearly one-fifth to about one-tenth.

TABLE 4.1: DISTRICT-WISE DISTRIBUTION OF EMIGRANTS, 1980 AND 1998

District	*1980 (in 1,000)*		*1998 (in 1,000)*	
Thiruvananthapuram	21.1	(11.3)	144.3	(10.4)
Kollam	18.8	(10.1)	225.7	(16.3)*
Alleppey	17.0	(9.1)	89.4	(6.5)
Kottayam	4.2	(2.2)	70.4	(5.1)
Idukki	0.3	(0.2)	12.6	(0.9)
Ernakulam	3.8	(2.0)	79.3	(5.7)
Trichur	37.9	(20.3)	147.7	(10.7)
Palakkad	7.0	(3.8)	67.9	(4.9)
Malappuram	34.8	(18.6)	239.0	(17.3)
Calicut	17.1	(9.2)	118.9	(8.6)
Kannur	24.6	(13.2)	188.4	(13.6)#
Total	186.5	(100.0)	1383.6	(100.0)

Notes: * Pathanamthitta and Kollam.
Kasargod, Kannur and Wayanad.

Age Composition

The age composition of return emigrants on the eve of their departure to the Middle East remained more or less unchanged. The numbers who were below 20 years of age or over 45 years of age was less than 14 per cent in 1985 and 11 per cent in 2001. In 2001, the proportion of emigrants above the age of 45 years was as low as 1.8 per cent. In 2001, on the other hand, nearly 30 per cent of the returnees were above the age of 45.

General Education

There was a significant improvement in general educational levels of return emigrants. In 1985, around 55 per cent had very low educational levels, say, lower primary schooling or less; in 2001 their numbers had declined to less than 20 per cent. Correspondingly, the proportion of emigrants who had completed secondary school had gone up from 18 per cent to 33 per cent during the period. Similarly, the proportion of return emigrants who had passed SSLC or had higher education increased from 24 per cent in 1985 to more than 40 per cent in 2001. Clearly, there was a steady improvement in the average educational status of emigrants over the past two decades.

Employment Status

The vast majority of return emigrants had been engaged in some sort of employment at the time of their emigration. In 1985, 38 per cent were unemployed and the corresponding figure in 2001 was 15 per cent, indicating that unemployment as a reason for emigration had diminished in importance over the years. However, economic reasons have been at the root of emigration in most of the cases not merely to get employment as such, but to secure a worthwhile job so as to improve their economic status.

Occupational Status

The occupational status of return emigrants prior to emigration, according to the 2001 survey, revealed some significant changes during the period under review. In 1985, around two-fifths of emigrants had little work experience on the eve of emigration; the corresponding figure for 2001 was 5 per cent. Similarly, in 1985, only 55 per cent had work experience in artisan trades and other services such as merchants, farmers, fishermen, transport and army and police, the corresponding figure in 2001 was over 85 per cent. In both years, the proportion of professional, managerial, administrative and technical personnel was around 6 per cent. Thus, there was a rising demand for middle level occupations requiring technical skills and work experience in the destination countries for emigrants from Kerala.

Earnings and Marital Status

The structure of the earning status of emigrants according to their marital status, on the eve of their first emigration, underwent a significant change during the period under review as clearly revealed in Table 4.2.

The years 1985 and 2001 are not strictly comparable in money terms. However, there was a significant change in the structure. For instance, in 1985, both married and unmarried emigrants

TABLE 4.2: RETURN EMIGRANTS BY MONTHLY INCOME AND MARITAL STATUS ON THE EVE OF THEIR FIRST EMIGRATION (IN %)

Monthly Income (Rs.)	*1985*		*2001*	
	Unmarried	*Married*	*Unmarried*	*Married*
< 100	72.5	30.7	–	3.3
100- 500	22.2	53.8	14.5	16.6
500- 1,000	3.2	10.3	40.0	35.6
1,000-2,000	1.7	4.9	29.1	29.8
2,000 and >	0.3	0.3	16.4	14.8

belonged predominantly to the low income groups; in contrast, in 2001 the low and high income categories were fairly small and the bulk of both married and unmarried, emigrants were from the middle income groups. This suggests that emigration costs were prohibitive for the very poor and the relatively well-off sections of the population were not enamoured by the prospects of employment and income in the Gulf countries.

AGE AND INCOME

The distribution of return emigrants by age and income status in 1985 and 2001 reveals an interesting trend (Table 4.3). The data presented in Table 4.3 substantiate those given in Table 4.2. While there was an upward movement in income in all the age groups, the increase was however to a limited extent. Even in 2003 the numbers in the income group of Rs. 2,000 and above were few not more than one-fifth in any age group with the exception of the 45-60 years age group. Another interesting observation is that emigrants in the higher income groups were also in the higher age groups; this phenomenon was more evident in 2001 than in 1985. Similarly, the structure in 2001 revealed a bulge in the middle income groups (unlike in 1985), except for the highest age group of 45-60 years.

INCOME BY RELIGION

The change over time in the income status of return emigrants on the eve of their first emigration was evident in all the major religious groups (Table 4.4). Among Hindus and Muslims, the

TABLE 4.3: DISTRIBUTION OF RETURN EMIGRANTS ACCORDING TO AGE GROUPS AND MONTHLY INCOME LEVELS ON THE EVE OF EMIGRATION: 1985 AND 2001

Monthly Income (Rs.)	*Age on the Eve of First Migration*										*Total*	
	< 20 Years		*20-25 Years*		*25-35 Years*		*35-45 Years*		*45-60 Years*			
	1985	*2001*	*1985*	*2001*	*1985*	*2001*	*1985*	*2001*	*1985*	*2001*	*1985*	*2001*
<100	87.3	4.3	68.4	3	42.4	2.1	27.3	0.7	34.4	–	51.7	2.1
100-200	7.9	4.3	9.5	–	22.5	1.1	22.3	1.3	13.8	–	16.7	1.0
200-500	4.8	29.8	14.0	17.8	28.2	14.6	28.9	16.3	17.2	6.7	21.2	16.5
500-1,000	–	25.5	5.9	39.6	4.6	37.1	14.0	32.7	17.2	13.3	6.8	35.8
1,000-2,000	–	27.7	1.8	30.2	1.9	29.4	7.4	30.1	17.2	26.7	3.3	29.6
2,000 and >	–	8.5	0.5	9.4	1.4	15.6	–	19.0	–	53.3	0.3	15.0
Total	100.0	100.0	100.0	100.0	100.0	100.0	100.0	100.0	100.0	100.0	100.0	100.0

TABLE 4.4: DISTRIBUTION OF HOUSEHOLDS BY RANGE OF ANNUAL INCOME ACCORDING TO RELIGION

Annual Income Class	*Religion*						
	Hindu		*Muslim*		*Christian*		
	1985	*2001*	*1985*	*2001*	*1985*	*2001*[a]	*2001*[b]
Low	25.2	14.2	20.3	10.8	14.8	13.6	10.4
Lower Middle	23.0	54.7	20.9	59.8	5.9	44.5	20.8
Upper Middle	20.7	24.1	35.9	25.2	17.6	26.4	58.3
High	31.0	6.9	22.9	4.2	61.7	15.5	10.4

Notes: [a]For Syrian Christians only.
[b]For Latin Christians only.

number of emigrants from the low and high income groups declined significantly while the proportion of the middle income group increased. In the case of Christians, the decline in the proportion of emigrants in the high income group was unexpectedly large. As indicated earlier, the lure of the Gulf countries for the relatively rich sections of the population in Kerala is rapidly waning probably because of the fall in income levels of expatriates in that region.

Reason for Emigration

The most important reason for emigration cited by most of the respondents, irrespective of religion, educational status and income status, both in 1985 and 2001 was lack of employment opportunities at home (or conversely, the desire for getting a job) (Table 4.5).

The need to secure a job assumed greater significance over time. This need was higher among the low educational and low income groups. The need to improve standards of living as the main reason for emigration was weak in the 1985 survey and it became weaker still in the 2001 survey. Repayment of debts was the greatest motive for emigration for less than 10 per cent of return emigrants in all religious groups. In 1985, the numbers who perceived this as the most important reason were fewer among all these groups. In 2001, it was cited as the most important reason by around one-seventh of the respondents in the 'below

TABLE 4.5: DISTRIBUTION OF EMIGRANTS BY THE MOST IMPORTANT REASON FOR EMIGRATION

	% of Emigrants Reporting as the Most Important Reason												*Total*	
	Lack of Employment Opportunity in Kerala (to Get a Job Abroad)		*To Improve Living Standards*		*To repay Debts*		*To discharge Responsi-bilities*		*To Accumulate Funds for Investment*		*For Enjoyment and Other Purposes*			
	1985	*2001*	*1985*	*2001*	*1985*	*2001*	*1985*	*2001*	*1985*	*2001*	*1985*	*2001*	*1985*	*2001*
(a) Religion														
Hindu	54.0	72.1	23.0	8.2	5.7	9.8	14.9	4.9	–	2.5	2.4	2.4	100.0	100.0
Muslim	43.4	79.9	22.0	2.4	2.2	10.1	29.9	4.7	0.6	1.2	1.9	1.8	100.0	100.0
Syrian Christian	47.0	58.6	32.4	27.6	5.9	–	14.7	4.2	–	1.7	1.7	10.3	100.0	100.0
Latin Christian	47.0	58.3	32.4	8.3	5.9	8.3	14.7	–	–	16.7	1.7	4.2	100.0	100.0
(b) Educational Status														
Below Primary (Including Illiterate)	19.6	88	17.4	4.0	4.3	4.0	54.4	–	–	4.0	4.3	–	100.0	100.0
Primary	39.3	81.4	23.9	–	3.9	9.3	31.1	7.0	–	2.3	1.8	–	100.0	100.0
Below Secondary	55.0	69.6	17.2	6.2	3.3	13.7	21.9	5.0	1.3	2.5	1.3	3.1	100.0	100.0
Secondary	60.0	74.4	22.2	12.4	0.8	3.9	14.3	3.1	0.8	1.6	1.6	4.7	100.0	100.0
College Educated	21.0	42.9	43.5	33.3	–	–	26.3	–	–	9.5	–	14.3	100.0	100.0

(Contd.)

TABLE 4.5 (Contd.)

	% of Emigrants Reporting as the Most Important Reason												Total	
	Lack of Employment Opportunity in Kerala (to Get a Job Abroad)		*To Improve Living Standards*		*To repay Debts*		*To discharge Responsi-bilities*		*To Accumulate Funds for Investment*		*For Enjoyment and Other Purposes*			
	1985	*2001*	*1985*	*2001*	*1985*	*2001*	*1985*	*2001*	*1985*	*2001*	*1985*	*2001*	*1985*	*2001*
(c) Monthly Income (Rs.)														
< 100	68.3	60.0	17.3	40.0	1.5	–	10.6	–	0.6	–	1.7	–	100.0	100.0
100-200	26.3	100.0	31.6	–	5.3	–	36.8	–	–	–	–	–	100.0	100.0
200-500	26.7	75.0	19.8	7.1	4.3	14.3	48.3	3.6	–	–	0.9	–	100.0	100.0
500-1,000	20.9	80.4	25.7	9.3	6.1	5.2	44.6	3.1	–	2.1	2.7	–	100.0	100.0
1,000-2,000	13.1	67.1	55.3	9.8	2.1	7.3	25.5	6.1	–	9.8	4.0	–	100.0	100.0
2,000 >	28.0	57.8	36.0	14.1	–	20.3	32	6.3	4.0	–	–	1.6	100.0	100.0

secondary' educational category. Further, in 2001, around one-fifth of return emigrants in the highest income group of Rs. 2,000 and above reported repayment of loans as the most important reason for emigration. Interestingly, no respondent in the 1985 survey had cited this as the most important reason.

COST OF EMIGRATION

The costs of emigration have been continually increasing over the past thirty years. According to the 1985 survey, nearly 90 per cent of emigrants prior to 1970 had spent less than Rs. 5,000 on emigration. Owing to monetary inflation in India as well as increasing difficulties of emigration due to procedural formalities, increase in the number of likely emigrants, costs have been rising steadily. The cumulative distribution of households according to money costs incurred per emigrant by time periods is presented in Table 4.6. In the table, data for the period prior to 1985 are drawn from the 1985 survey and data for the period beginning 1985 are taken from the 2001 survey. The two sets of data are

TABLE 4.6: CUMULATIVE DISTRIBUTION OF HOUSEHOLDS ACCORDING TO MONEY COSTS INCURRED PER EMIGRANT BY PERIOD OF EMIGRATION (%)

Period	*Less than Rs. 500*	*Less than Rs. 1,000*	*Less than Rs. 5,000*	*Less than Rs. 10,000*	*Less than Rs. 15,000*	*Less than Rs. 20,000*	*Less than Rs. 25,000*	*Less than Rs. 50,000*	*More than Rs. 50,000*
				According to 1985 Survey					
Before 1970	21.3	46.6	89.3	97.3	97.3	98.6	100		
1970-2	7.5	23.9	80.6	97.0	98.5	98.5	98.5	100	
1973-5	4.6	13.8	55.1	82.6	97.3	98.2	100		
1975-0	1.9	4.4	28.0	53.8	76.4	91.4	96.8	100	
1980-5	0.8	1.6	11.5	33.6	47.3	76.3	92.3	99.2	100
				According to 2001 Survey					
1985-90	2.86	2.86	5.24	8.57	14.76	23.81	33.81	82.86	100
1990-5	2.05	2.40	3.42	5.82	8.56	13.70	21.58	66.10	100
1995-2000	3.06	5.10	5.10	5.10	9.18	14.29	20.41	53.06	100

not strictly comparable in terms of specific numbers, however, the trend of rising costs is discernible in both.

During the latest quinquennial period (1995-2000), around 14 per cent of emigrants had incurred expenses less than Rs. 20,000; nearly 40 per cent had spent between Rs. 20,000 and Rs. 50,000; and around 47 per cent had spent more than Rs. 50,000. Throughout the period the costs of emigration have remained in general lower for the highly educated than for the illiterate or the lowly educated. This fact was more evident in the 1985 survey than in the 2001 survey (see Table 4.7).

According to the 1985 survey, around two-thirds of the emigrants' households had spent Rs. 10,000 or less on emigration. As mentioned earlier, the proportion decreased with an increase in the educational level of the emigrant. For example, around 39 per cent of emigrants who were illiterate or had less than primary education were able to limit their expenses to under Rs. 10,000. The corresponding percentage in the case of those with primary education was around 70, and 79 for the college educated including degree holders.

In the 2001 survey, the differences across educational categories were blurred because of the demand in the Gulf countries for expatriate workers with higher educational qualifications. For instance, while less than 30 per cent of emigrants as a whole limited their emigration expenses to less than Rs. 20,000, the corresponding percentage for the highly educated (college education including graduates and postgraduates) was 45. Surprisingly, the corresponding figure for the least educated was also high. Obviously, the pressure for emigration was from groups of emigrants who had moderate levels of education, i.e. above primary school and below SSLC.

Sources of Financing

There was an interesting change in the sources of financing emigration. In the 1985 survey it was observed that around 43 per cent of emigration costs had been financed by the savings of the migrants themselves or of their parents, the corresponding figure in the 2001 survey was 27 per cent. Similarly, while only 15 per cent of emigration costs had been met, according to the

TABLE 4.7: CUMULATIVE DISTRIBUTION OF HOUSEHOLDS BY MONEY COSTS INCURRED PER EMIGRANT ACCORDING TO LEVEL OF EDUCATION

Educational Level	*Cost of Emigration*																*Total*	
	Less than Rs. 500		*Less than Rs. 1,000*		*Less than Rs. 5,000*		*Less than Rs. 10,000*		*Less than Rs. 15,000*		*Less than Rs. 20,000*		*Less than Rs. 25,000*		*Less than Rs. 50,000*			
	1985	*2001*	*1985*	*2001*	*1985*	*2001*	*1985*	*2001*	*1985*	*2001*	*1985*	*2001*	*1985*	*2001*	*1985*	*2001*	*1985*	*2001*
Illiterate and Below Primary	6.5	1.9	10.9	3.8	23.9	9.4	39.1	18.9	54.3	32.1	80.4	45.3	100	58.5		83.0		100.0
Primary	4.8	3.2	12.4	3.2	45.6	6.4	69.5	12.7	82.3	17.5	92.8	23.8	97.6	35.7	99.7	80.2	100.0	100.0
Secondary Including SSLC Holders	6.0	5.1	10.6	5.7	37.1	9.0	61.6	11.8	76.8	22.0	89.4	30.7	96	39.5	100.0	80.1		100.0
College Educated	4.4	5.1	15.8	5.1	47.4	12.8	79.0	23.1	89.5	33.3	100.0	44.9		51.3		83.3		100.0
Total	4.7	3.4	11.7	3.9	40.7	6.9	63.3	12.0	78.5	20.5	91.0	29.8	96.9	39.7	96.9	78.5	100.0	100.0

TABLE 4.8: SOURCES OF EMIGRATION COSTS

Sources	*1985 Survey*	*2001 Survey*
Personal Savings and Parents' Savings	43.2	27.0
Borrowings:		
From Friends and Relatives (Interest Free Loans)	31.8	33.0
From Banks	3.4	2.9
From Moneylenders	4.9	8.2
Sale/Mortgage of Property, Jewellery and Financial Assets	14.8	28.3
Government Assistance	1.9	0.7
Total	100.0	100.0

1985 survey, from the sale of physical assets such as property, ornaments and jewellery and from financial assets, the corresponding proportion according to the 2001 survey was as high as 28 per cent. The role of the government in providing aid to meet the costs of emigration has been extremely limited, less than 2 per cent in both the surveys (Table 4.8).

Type of Employment Contract

Till the early 1980s, emigration to the Gulf countries was more a free enterprise than an activity regulated by the government. Since the mid-1980s, the situation greatly improved with a decline in the number of emigrants leaving the country in search of employment in the Middle East without formal contract agreements. However, emigration with informal contracts (or with no contracts) has continued as revealed by the 2001 survey (Table 4.9).

TABLE 4.9: EMIGRANTS BY TYPE OF CONTRACT (%)

Type of Contract	*1985*	*2001*
Formal Contract (Specifying Terms and Conditions of:		
Work and Living	24.3	47.8
Letter from Employer	5.2	7.1
Informal Arrangements	66.7	44.3
Others	3.8	0.7

Interestingly, as revealed by the 2001 survey, nearly 45 per cent of emigrants went abroad without valid employment contracts. Even today there is large scale clandestine emigration from Kerala, it is likely that it is supported by fraudulent travel documents.

B. THE MIGRATION PHASE: WORKING AND LIVING CONDITIONS ABROAD

WORKING CONDITIONS

The process of emigration became more methodical and streamlined after the revision of emigration rules in India in 1984. Earlier, the majority of emigrants did not have any clear idea about the nature and conditions of work in the host countries, largely because they travelled abroad without proper employment contracts or definite job expectations. Therefore, they were not disillusioned if they found inferior jobs, low wages, poor working conditions or little job security. On the basis of the 1985 survey, it was observed: 'Since a large proportion (about 75 per cent) of the migrants have proceeded without formal contracts, without specific jobs in mind, and without hope of comfortable working conditions, there was little disappointment among most of them about the terms and conditions of work they eventually received'. Obviously, they had little option in the matter. The 2001 survey showed, on the other hand, that more than two-thirds of return emigrants were satisfied that they had been given the same jobs, which had been promised to them at the time of recruitment.

According to the 1985 survey, more than two-thirds of return emigrants were of the opinion that the conditions of their employment were better than those in other countries, the corresponding proportion in the 2001 survey was about one-fourth. During the interim period job expectations had undergone serious upward revision. The vast majority was, however, satisfied that the conditions were not less favourable for them. Only about one-fourth were of the opinion that there was some discrimination against expatriates from Kerala. However, it seems that the employment conditions in the Gulf countries have been in general non-discriminatory towards expatriate workers from the different

Asian countries and Keralites by and large have been satisfied in this respect.

LIVING CONDITIONS

Living conditions refer to housing, food, facilities for entertainment, recreation, travel, medical care and education. According to the 1985 survey, less than 10 per cent of emigrants faced problems related to passport, visas, work permits, etc. The magnitude of such problems was higher according to the 2001 survey. Nearly nine of every ten respondents reported that they were not allowed to keep their passports with them. Less than one-eighth of emigrants were accompanied by their spouses in both the surveys.

Housing conditions were described as good or satisfactory by over four-fifths of the respondents in both the surveys. Only those who were employed in very lowly jobs described housing conditions as poor or inadequate. The proportion of those who were dissatisfied was higher in the 1985 survey (about 25 per cent) than in the 2001 survey (below 10 per cent). Housing conditions of expatriate workers from Kerala have somewhat improved over the years.

With regard to the quality of food also, the number who perceived it as poor was barely one-eighth in the 1985 survey and around one-sixteenth in the 2001 survey. Nor was the cost of food reported to be high.

Most of the respondents in both the surveys were satisfied with the facilities for entertainment; this was true of all the destination countries. The proportion of dissatisfied was less than 20 per cent. Entertainment included listening to radio, viewing television and going to the cinema. Facilities for sports, picnics and tours were, however, for more limited and restricted.

Around one-sixth of the respondents in both the surveys complained about the availability and quality of medical facilities. According to the 2001 survey, nearly 8 per cent of the respondents reported lack of medical facilities at their work places. It is likely that they were engaged in low level jobs in desert camps or in remote uninhabited areas.

Educational facilities were not a major concern for most of the respondents as their families had stayed back home. However, the general impression of the vast majority (over 75 per cent) was that the facilities were good or at least adequate. However, the 2001 survey revealed that the subsidies to expatriates for food, medical aid and education were being slowly withdrawn in most of the Gulf countries.

According to the 1985 survey, workers rarely contacted the Indian embassies and consulates in the host countries. Only 4 per cent had contacted them on arrival and a mere 6 per cent had contacted them at the time of departure. The major reason for such apathy on the part of the emigrants was reportedly the ineffectiveness of these agencies in redressing their grievances and solving their problems. The situation has not improved greatly since then. According to the 2001 survey, less than 10 per cent had sought assistance from the embassies or consulates.

Adjustment Problems

During the absence of the emigrants from home, the responsibility of managing the household fell on their spouses, parents, relatives or close friends. The overall picture that emerged from both the surveys was that adjustment was not much of a problem. In nearly 55 per cent of the households where the emigrants were unmarried, the households were managed by their parents, as had been the case even prior to emigration. In 25 per cent of the households the spouses (mostly wives) had to shoulder the responsibility according to the 1985 survey, whereas the corresponding figure in the 2001 survey was as high as 40 per cent. Correspondingly, there was a decline in the proportion of households which were managed by relatives or friends (from 20 per cent to 6 per cent). It is likely that during the interim period, the proportion of nuclear households had increased and wives had become more confident in handling household affairs without assistance (Table 4.10).

In both the surveys the proportion of households which reported that they could not handle the responsibility of household management in the absence of the emigrant was negligible.

TABLE 4.10: RESPONSIBILITY FOR MANAGING HOUSEHOLDS OF EMIGRANTS

Agency	%	
	1985 Survey	*2001 Survey*
Spouse	25	40
Emigrants' Parents	55	54
Parents of Spouse and Other Relatives	18	2
Others Including Friends	2	4

REMITTANCES

Economic goals being the major motivation for emigration, the primary concern of all emigrants was remittance to their households. According to the 1985 survey, 98 per cent had succeeded in saving some money. Almost all these emigrants had made periodical remittances of all or part of their savings to their households. The situation did not change much in 2001, as it was found that over 90 per cent of the respondents made remittances on a regular basis. Remittances were in the form of bank drafts to spouses or parents, further, less than 5 per cent sent money to others in both the surveys. Less than 20 per cent deposited a part of their savings in NRI accounts in India in 1985 and 2001.

Instances of being cheated in the course of making remittances were few in both the surveys; around 4 per cent in the 1985 survey and a little over 2 per cent in the 2001 survey. In the 2001 survey, it was found that the agencies which cheated included friends and relatives as well as non-banking financial dealers.

REASONS FOR RETURN

The most important reasons for return were expiry of contract, termination of job by the employer, difficult working and living conditions and compulsory repatriation by the host government. The relative importance of these reasons has changed over time. However, the figures available from the two surveys are not strictly comparable. Instances of arbitrary termination of job by the employer and compulsory repatriation by the government have declined over the years (Table 4.11).

TABLE 4.11: REASONS FOR RETURN

Reason	%	
	1985 Survey	*2001 Survey**
Expiry of Contract	24.3	30.3
Difficult Living Conditions Including Ill-health, Injury	6.5	25.2
Difficult Working Conditions	8.1	22.9
Job Terminated by Employer	31.8	10.3
Compulsory Repatriation by Government	19.8	7.3
Problems at Home	9.5	13.7

Note: * Percentages not added up to 100 as there was more than one reason in many cases.

C. POST-RETURN PHASE

In the 1985 survey, it was observed,

> There does not exist in Kerala any agency—governmental, institutional or voluntary—to deal with the problem of the rehabilitation of returned migrants. There is no agency or arrangement to help with the retraining or placement of these persons, and they have to fall back on friends and of relatives, though in the majority of cases even this source was not of great help. The assistance rendered by friends and relatives included advice about employment (including self-employment) opportunities and sources of finance.

However, the situation at the time of the 2001 survey was markedly different. There were hundreds of associations of return migrants and the Kerala government had set up a separate department in 1997 to look into the problems of rehabilitation of return emigrants. Despite the emergence of large numbers of associations, there was no significant change in the conditions which emigrants had to cope with on their return to Kerala.

According to the 1985 survey, around 60 per cent of return emigrants were unemployed and about 2 per cent had retired from active work. Of the remaining, nearly 39 per cent, who were engaged in some sort of economic activity, 25 per cent were self-employed. The situation was greatly different in 2001: the proportion of the unemployed had declined to below 8 per cent and that of the employed had increased to 73 per cent, around 44 per cent of them were self-employed.

The 1985 survey revealed that not many return emigrants were willing to make investments in industry or business in Kerala because of lack of finances, labour unrest, raw material shortages, dearth of technical competence, fear of government intervention and marketing problems.

Even though the employment opportunities of return emigrants had improved in 2001, most of them preferred relatively low investment ventures such as agricultural labour and transport and other service sectors. Manufacturing industries provided employment to less than 8 per cent of return emigrants. The fact that even in 2001 the vast majority had to turn to agriculture for employment indicated the undeveloped character of the economy. Unless the Kerala economy shows more dynamism in providing an investment-friendly climate, employment and income opportunities in the state for its job-seekers including return emigrants, would remain bleak.

CHAPTER 5

Emigration and Transitions in Economic Activity

The transitions in economic activity associated with emigration and return emigration are discussed here. The economic activity of return emigrants is examined at three stages—before emigration, during their stay abroad and after their return to Kerala. Further, the movements of workers across industrial sectors at the various stages of transition—from Kerala to the Gulf countries and from the Gulf countries back home—are investigated and a measure of the overall inter-sector mobility is presented.

Work Experience of Return Emigrants Before Emigration

Prior to their first emigration, 17 per cent of return emigrants had been self-employed, 42 per cent held casual jobs and only 18.5 per cent had any regular employment (Table 5.1).

TABLE 5.1: ECONOMIC ACTIVITY OF RETURN EMIGRANTS BEFORE EMIGRATION

	%
Regular Employment	18.5
Casual Employment	42.2
Self-employment	17.2
Unemployed Seeking Work	13.0
Unemployed not Seeking Work	1.9
Others	7.2
Total	100.0

Source: Field survey, 2001.

Only 13 per cent of return emigrants had been unemployed at the time of their first emigration. In 1998, the proportion of unemployed among those who had emigrated, was 26.5 per cent prior to their emigration (Zachariah, Mathew and Irudaya Rajan, 1999; Zachariah, Nair and Irudaya Rajan, 2001). Thus, it would appear that those who returned were a select group from the point of view of unemployment. Besides, a higher number of those who had some employment prior to their first emigration had returned.

Nearly 30 per cent of return emigrants had been engaged in production-related activities prior to emigration. It is likely that these people enhanced their technical knowledge and skills during their stay abroad and are capable of making an effective contribution to development activities. On the other hand, around 46 per cent had worked as farmers, fishermen, sales persons or petty shopkeepers abroad. They were able to make remittances home but were neither qualified nor skilled to contribute to the development activities in the state (Table 5.2).

As in the case of education, return emigrants were a selected group from emigrants in the Gulf countries as far as occupation was concerned. The proportion of unemployed persons seeking jobs among them was 7.89 times the corresponding proportion on the eve of first emigration, among emigrants still working abroad. A smaller number of return emigrants held white-collar

TABLE 5.2: OCCUPATIONAL DISTRIBUTION OF RETURN EMIGRANTS PRIOR TO FIRST EMIGRATION (TOTAL 794)

Occupation	%
Teacher/Professor	4.8
Paramedical staff	1.6
Sculptors/Musicians	0.3
Office Workers/Clerks	2.8
Salesmen/Merchants	17.4
Farmers/Fishermen	28.5
Production-related Workers	30.9
Transport Workers	8.8
Unemployed Students	5.0
Total	100.0

Source: Zachariah, Mathew and Irudaya Rajan, 2003.

TABLE 5.3: OCCUPATION OF EMIGRANTS IN THE GULF COUNTRIES AND OF RETURN EMIGRANTS IN KERALA, 1998

Occupation	*EMI*	*REM*
Office Workers: Government Service	2.4	2.5
Semi-government Service	0.9	0.3
Private Sector	39.8	5.5
Self-employment	4.1	35.1
Unpaid Family Worker	0.0	1.3
Agricultural Labourer	0.1	4.3
Non-agricultural Labourer	47.5	27.6
Job Seekers	0.5	6.8
Job not Required	0.4	6.6
Student	1.6	2.3
HH Duties	2.7	7.0
Pensioners	–	0.5
Total	100.0	100.0

Source: Zachariah, Mathew and Irudaya Rajan, 2003.

jobs in government, semi-government and private sectors and were engaged in various other non-manual activities in the secondary and tertiary sectors as compared to the number of emigrants. On the other hand, the number of return emigrants who were self-employed, worked as agricultural labour and did household jobs (as well as those who had opted to lead a retired life or were seeking a job) was much larger (see Table 5.3).

Approximately 43 per cent of the emigrants held white-collar jobs in government, semi-government and private sectors. On other hand, only 8.3 per cent of return emigrants were engaged in such work.

Economic Sector Before Emigration

Emigrants and return emigrants were evenly distributed among the various economic sectors. Emigrants to the Gulf countries included workers from all economic classes. Around 23 per cent of return emigrants were drawn from agriculture and allied activities, 26 per cent from manufacturing and construction activities, 30 per cent from trade, commerce and transport and

15 per cent from other services. There was not much selectivity (in terms of economic sector) as far as emigration was concerned. Any healthy person with the right contacts could be an emigrant as the demand was largely for unskilled work (Table 5.4).

TABLE 5.4: ECONOMIC SECTOR IN KERALA BEFORE EMIGRATION

Sector	%
Agriculture Animal Husbandry	22.3
Mining/Quarrying	0.9
Manufacturing	7.6
Construction	18.2
Trade, Commerce, Hotels	18.6
Transport	11.0
Other Services	15.4
Others	6.1
Total	100.0

Source: Field survey, 2001.

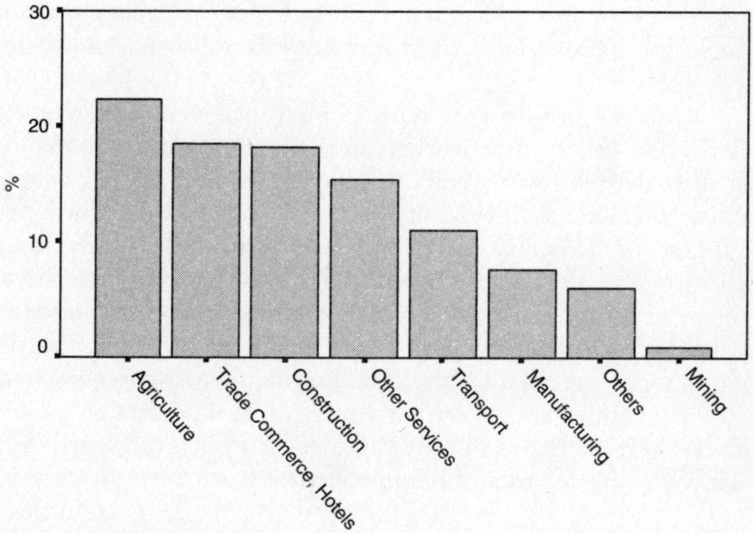

Source: Field survey, 2001.

FIGURE 5.1: RETURN EMIGRANTS BY INDUSTRIAL SECTOR BEFORE EMIGRATION

TABLE 5.5: OCCUPATION OF RETURN EMIGRANTS IN THE GULF

Occupation	*Before Emigration*	*After Emigration*
Teacher/Professor	4.8	4.7
Paramedical Staff	1.6	1.9
Sculptors/Musicians	0.3	8.5
Office Workers/Clerks	2.8	36.8
Salesmen/Merchants	17.4	11.3
Farmers/Fishermen	28.5	23.6
Production-related Workers	30.9	8.5
Transport Workers	8.8	4.7
Unemployed, Students	5.0	0.0
	100.0	100.0

Source: Field survey, 2001.

Work Experience Acquired by Return Emigrants in the Gulf Countries

The Gulf economy is qualitatively different from the basically agrarian economy of Kerala. Therefore, considerable change in the sector of economic activity was expected following emigration (see Table 5.5).

Nearly 37 per cent of return emigrants were employed as clerks and other office workers in the Gulf countries on the eve of their departure to Kerala. Interestingly, only 2.8 per cent of them had done such type of work in Kerala prior to their first emigration. This change, an increase of around 34 percentage points, was the largest observed in the activity transition consequent on emigration. It was from the category of production-related workers that the bulk of persons were recruited as office workers, as revealed by the decrease the former category from 30.9 per cent to 8.5 per cent, a decline of 22.4 percentage points. There were increases in only three occupations: office workers, sculptors, musicians and paramedical staff.

Sectors of Employment in the Gulf Countries

Consequent on emigration, a significant shift was observed in the employment sectors of emigrants, from the primary to the secondary and tertiary sectors. While around 23 per cent of emigrants were engaged in agriculture and allied activities prior to emigration, only 6 per cent were employed in these sectors abroad. There was not much change in the proportion engaged in manufacturing; it was around 7.5 per cent at both the stages. Construction, however, accounted for a higher percentage in the Gulf countries: 25 per cent as against 18 per cent in Kerala. In the services sector, transport registered a decline, whereas, other services registered an increase (see Table 5.6).

TABLE 5.6: ECONOMIC SECTOR (IN THE GULF) OF EMPLOYED RETURN EMIGRANTS

	Kerala	*Gulf*
Agricultural Animal Husbandry	22.3	4.5
Mining/Quarrying	0.9	1.5
Manufacturing	7.6	7.4
Construction	18.2	24.8
Trade, Commerce, Hotels	18.6	25.5
Transport	11.0	7.6
Other Services	15.4	20.3
Others	6.1	8.4
Total	100.0	100.0

Source: Field survey, 2001.

TRANSITIONS IN ECONOMIC ACTIVITY

A detailed account of the transition of workers by the industrial sector of activity consequent on emigration is presented in Table 5.7. For example, only 15.8 per cent of return emigrants who had been engaged in agriculture and animal husbandry prior to emigration were employed in this sector in the Gulf countries. The major shifts from this sector were to construction, trade, commerce and hotels, and other services. There were sizeable shifts to construction and other services from other sub-sectors as well. As seen in Table 5.8, of the 100 return emigrants who were employed in the agricultural sector in the Gulf countries, about 71 per cent were those who had been working in this sector prior to emigration. Similarly, of the 100 return emigrants in the manufacturing sector in the Gulf countries, 42.9 per cent

TABLE 5.7: TRANSITIONS IN ACTIVITY CONSEQUENT ON EMIGRATION

In the Gulf	*In Kerala*								
	1	*2*	*3*	*4*	*5*	*6*	*7*	*8*	*Total*
1	15.8	0.0	3.4	0.7	0.7	2.4	3.4	2.1	5.0
2	0.6	0.0	5.2	0.7	1.4	1.2	2.5	0.0	1.4
3	1.8	28.6	41.4	3.6	3.5	6.1	5.9	10.6	7.3
4	21.1	14.3	20.7	77.0	10.6	12.2	10.2	23.4	26.7
5	33.3	14.3	8.6	5.8	55.6	12.2	12.7	17.0	24.0
6	5.3	14.3	1.7	0.7	5.6	46.3	4.2	2.1	8.4
7	17.0	28.6	12.1	5.8	19.0	13.4	55.1	14.9	20.4
8	5.3	0.0	6.9	5.8	3.5	6.1	5.9	29.8	6.8
Total	100.0	100.0	100.0	100.0	100.0	100.0	100.0	100.0	100.0

Note: 1 = agriculture; 2 = mining, etc; 3 = manufacturing; 4 = construction; 5 = trade, commerce, etc; 6 = transport; 7 = other services; 8 = others.

Source: Field survey, 2001.

TABLE 5.8 INDUSTRIAL DISTRIBUTION OF WORKERS IN THE GULF COUNTRIES ACCORDING TO THEIR ACTIVITIES IN KERALA PRIOR TO EMIGRATION

In the Gulf	*In Kerala*								
	1	*2*	*3*	*4*	*5*	*6*	*7*	*8*	*Total*
1	71.1	0.0	5.3	2.6	2.6	5.3	10.5	2.6	100
2	9.1	0.0	27.3	9.1	18.2	9.1	27.3	0.0	100
3	5.4	3.6	42.9	8.9	8.9	8.9	12.5	8.9	100
4	17.6	0.5	5.9	52.5	7.4	4.9	5.9	5.4	100
5	31.1	0.5	2.7	4.4	43.2	5.5	8.2	4.4	100
6	14.1	1.6	1.6	1.6	12.5	59.4	7.8	1.6	100
7	18.6	1.3	4.5	5.1	17.3	7.1	41.7	4.5	100
8	17.3	0.0	7.7	15.4	9.6	9.6	13.5	26.9	100
Total	22.4	0.9	7.6	18.2	18.6	10.7	15.4	6.2	100

Note: 1 = agriculture; 2 = mining, etc; 3 = manufacturing; 4 = construction; 5 = trade, commerce, etc; 6 = transport; 7 = other services; 8 = others.

Source: Field survey, 2001.

had been in this sector in Kerala; of the 100 who were in trade and commerce, 31 had been in agriculture in Kerala; 17.6 per cent had shifted from agriculture to construction.

The question arises have the return emigrants adopted their original economic activity after coming back from abroad? Some of the emigrants have, but most of them have not. Upon their return there was a considerable change in their economic activity from what they had in the Gulf countries.

ECONOMIC ACTIVITY AFTER RETURN

Nearly three-fourths of return emigrants were gainfully employed in Kerala at the time of the study and around 8 per cent were actively seeking employment. Including the unemployed who were not seeking employment, 19.4 per cent were outside the labour force (Table 5.9). Of the return emigrants who were employed, 44 per cent were self-employed and almost a similar percentage were casual labourers. Only 14 per cent had regular employment (Table 5.10).

TABLE 5.9: ECONOMIC ACTIVITY OF RETURN EMIGRANTS IN KERALA

Economic Activity in 2001	%
Gainfully Employed/Employee	72.7
Unemployed Seeking Employment	7.9
Unemployed not Seeking Employment	3.3
Not in Labour Force	16.1
Total	100.0

Source: Field survey, 2001.

TABLE 5.10: GAINFULLY EMPLOYED RETURN EMIGRANTS BY ECONOMIC STATUS

	%
Regular Employment	14.2
Casual Employment	41.6
Self-employment	44.2
Total	100.0

Source: Field survey, 2001.

Around one-fourth of the gainfully employed return emigrants were engaged in the agricultural sector and an equal number was engaged in trade, commerce and hotels. These two sectors together accounted for 49 per cent of the total gainfully employed return emigrants. Construction and transport were the other sectors in which return emigrants were employed. Each of these sectors employed nearly 15 per cent of the total. In the manufacturing sector, around 8 per cent of the economically active return emigrants were employed, indicating the industrial backwardness of the State (Table 5.11).

TABLE 5.11: GAINFULLY EMPLOYED RETURN EMIGRANTS BY ECONOMIC STATUS

Economic Sector	*Kerala Before Emigration*	*Gulf after Emigration*	*Kerala after Return*
Agriculture Animal Husbandry	22.3	4.5	24.8
Mining/Quarrying	0.9	1.5	0.2
Manufacturing	7.6	7.4	7.6
Construction	18.2	24.8	15.3
Trade, Commerce, Hotels	18.6	25.5	23.8
Transport	11.0	7.6	14.4
Other Services	15.4	20.3	8.4
Others	6.1	8.4	5.5
Total	100.0	100.0	100.0

Source: Field survey, 2001.

Significant changes were observed in the economic activity of return emigrants between their Gulf sojourn and post-return period in Kerala. For example, the proportion of workers in agriculture increased from 4.5 per cent to 24.8 per cent; it increased from 7.6 per cent to 14.4 per cent in transport. Correspondingly, there were major decreases in the other sectors. The proportion in other services fell from 20.3 per cent to 8.4 per cent and in construction from 24.8 per cent to 15.3 per cent. There were minor changes in the proportion of workers in manufacturing and trade.

It is clear from Table 5.12 that of those employed in agriculture in the Gulf, 75 per cent remained in agriculture after their return

TABLE 5.12: SECTOR OF ECONOMIC ACTIVITY IN THE GULF BY THAT IN KERALA AFTER RETURN

In Kerala after Return	*Economic Activity in Gulf Before Return*								
	1	*2*	*3*	*4*	*5*	*6*	*7*	*8*	*Total*
1	75.0	18.2	15.4	19.7	27.7	13.2	28.9	20.0	24.9
2	0.0	0.0	0.0	0.0	0.6	0.0	0.8	0.0	0.3
3	3.6	9.1	46.2	4.6	5.1	0.0	5.0	5.5	7.8
4	7.1	8.1	3.8	42.2	6.2	3.8	9.1	0.0	15.2
5	3.6	54.5	15.4	12.7	35.0	20.8	25.6	36.4	24.0
6	0.0	0.0	5.8	11.6	11.3	58.5	11.6	10.9	14.0
7	7.1	9.1	9.6	4.6	9.6	1.9	13.2	10.9	8.4
8	3.6	0.0	3.8	4.6	4.5	1.9	5.8	16.4	5.4
Total	100.0	100.0	100.0	100.0	100.0	100.0	100.0	100.0	100.0

Note: 1 = agriculture; 2 = mining, etc; 3 = manufacturing; 4 = construction; 5 = trade, commerce, etc; 6 = transport; 7 = other services; 8 = others.

Source: Field survey, 2001.

to Kerala. However, 7.1 per cent moved to construction and other services. Similarly, 15.4 per cent of those who were in manufacturing in the Gulf moved to agriculture and trade and commerce. While 35 per cent of those who were in trade and commerce remained in the same sector, 28 per cent moved to agriculture and 10 per cent to other services.

Viewed from the perspective of Kerala, it may be noted that out of 100 workers in agriculture after return, only 12.6 were in agriculture in the Gulf, 21 per cent were in other services and 20 per cent were in construction. There were significant shifts from the industrial sectors to agriculture on return from abroad (Table 5.13). Similarly, 50 per cent engaged in each of the primary sector activities such as mining and quarrying and fisheries had worked in trade and commerce and in other services in the Gulf. Similar inter-sectoral shifts were observed in all the sub-sectors.

In the final reckoning, has emigration led to any real change in the economic sectors of activity of return emigrants? It can be seen from Table 5.11 that prior to emigration, around 22 per cent of the labour force was engaged in agriculture. However,

TABLE 5.13: SECTOR OF ECONOMIC ACTIVITY IN KERALA AFTER RETURN BY ACTIVITY IN THE GULF

In Kerala after Return	*Economic Activity in Gulf Before Return*								
	1	*2*	*3*	*4*	*5*	*6*	*7*	*8*	*Total*
1	12.6	1.2	4.8	20.4	29.3	4.2	21.0	6.6	100.0
2	0.0	0.0	0.0	0.0	50.0	0.0	50.0	0.0	100.0
3	1.9	1.9	46.2	15.4	17.3	0.0	11.5	5.8	100.0
4	2.0	1.0	2.0	71.6	10.8	2.0	10.8	0.0	100.0
5	0.6	3.7	5.0	13.7	38.5	6.8	19.3	12.4	100.0
6	0.0	0.0	3.2	21.3	21.3	33.0	14.9	6.4	100.0
7	3.6	1.8	8.9	14.3	30.4	1.8	28.6	10.7	100.0
8	2.8	0.0	5.6	22.2	22.2	2.8	19.4	25.0	100.0
Total	4.2	1.6	7.8	25.8	26.4	7.9	18.1	8.2	100.0

Note: 1 = agriculture; 2 = mining, etc; 3 = manufacturing; 4 = construction; 5 = trade, commerce, etc; 6 = transport; 7 = other services; 8 = others.

Source: Field survey, 2001.

only 4.5 per cent of them remained in this sector in the Gulf. On their return many of those who had worked in sectors other than agriculture opted for employment in agriculture; the proportion of return emigrants engaged in agricultural activities was almost one-fourth. In other words, emigration had not made much impact on the proportion engaged in agriculture.

In the same manner, there was no change in the proportion of labour force working in manufacturing. Nearly 7.6 per cent of return emigrants were employed in manufacturing before emigration and after return. The proportion was more or less the same even during their sojourn in the Gulf. However, there was some increase in the proportion working in trade and commerce and in transport. This relative stability is somewhat misleading as it conceals the greater inter-sectoral mobility. The overall percentages conceal movements across sectors that would become clear only on closer scrutiny.

It is true that over two-thirds of those who had originally worked in agriculture remained in agriculture, but about 12 per cent moved to trade and commerce and 8 per cent to construction. Similarly, 55 per cent of those who were engaged in manufacturing before emigration remained in manufacturing after their return to Kerala. The remaining 45 per cent moved to other sectors: 14 per cent to agriculture, 14 per cent to trade, commerce, hotels, restaurants, etc., 7 per cent to services, 5 per cent to construction, etc. Almost 60 per cent of workers in trade and commerce remained in this sector, but 10 per cent moved to transport and 11 per cent to agriculture. Further, 73 per cent remained in transport, but 16 per cent moved to trade and commerce. Those who were engaged in other services before emigration exhibited maximum mobility: 18 per cent went to agriculture, 14 per cent to trade and commerce and 12 per cent to construction, etc.

In the foregoing analysis, the starting point was the situation in Kerala before emigration. The situation in Kerala after return was compared with that before emigration. Which industrial sectors did the return emigrants choose as opposed to the sectors to which they had belonged prior to emigration? An alternative approach would be to start from the situation after return to Kerala. For example, how many of those who were in agriculture after return to Kerala had moved from other sectors (see Tables 5.14 and 5.15).

TABLE 5.14: ECONOMIC SECTOR OF ACTIVITY OF RETURN EMIGRANTS BEFORE EMIGRATION AND IN KERALA AFTER RETURN

Return	*Before Emigration*								
Emigration	*1*	*2*	*3*	*4*	*5*	*6*	*7*	*8*	*Total*
1	68.9	16.7	14.3	12.9	11.2	4.3	17.9	13.9	24.8
2	0.8	0.0	0.0	0.0	0.9	0.0	0.0	0.0	0.3
3	4.5	16.7	54.8	2.6	4.3	0.0	6.4	16.7	8.2
4	3.0	33.3	4.8	62.1	5.2	0.0	11.5	5.6	16.3
5	12.1	0.0	14.3	10.3	60.3	15.7	14.1	27.8	22.8
6	8.3	33.3	2.4	6.0	9.5	72.9	5.1	5.6	14.9
7	2.3	0.0	7.1	0.9	4.3	5.7	34.6	8.3	7.7
8	0.0	0.0	2.4	5.2	4.3	1.4	10.3	22.2	4.9
Total	100.0	100.0	100.0	100.0	100.0	100.0	100.0	100.0	100.0

Note: 1 = agriculture; 2 = mining, etc; 3 = manufacturing; 4 = construction; 5 = trade, commerce, etc; 6 = transport; 7 = other services; 8 = others.

Source: Field survey, 2001.

TABLE 5.15: PER CENT OF RETURN EMIGRANTS IN AN ECONOMIC SECTOR WHO MOVED TO OTHER SECTORS BEFORE EMIGRATION AND AFTER RETURN TO KERALA

After Return	*Before Emigration* 1	2	3	4	5	6	7	8	*Total*
1	61.5	0.7	4.1	10.1	8.8	2.0	9.5	3.4	100.0
2	50.0	0.0	0.0	0.0	50.0	0.0	0.0	0.0	100.0
3	12.2	2.0	46.9	6.1	10.2	0.0	10.2	12.2	100.0
4	4.1	2.1	2.1	74.2	6.2	0.0	9.3	2.1	100.0
5	11.8	0.0	4.4	8.8	51.5	8.1	8.1	7.4	100.0
6	12.4	2.2	1.1	7.9	12.4	57.3	4.5	2.2	100.0
7	6.5	0.0	6.5	2.2	10.9	8.7	58.7	6.5	100.0
8	0.0	0.0	3.4	20.7	17.2	3.4	27.6	27.6	100.0
Total	22.1	1.0	7.0	19.5	19.5	11.7	13.1	6.0	100.0

Note: 1 = agriculture; 2 = mining, etc; 3 = manufacturing; 4 = construction; 5 = trade, commerce, etc; 6 = transport; 7 = other services; 8 = others.

Source: Field survey, 2001.

Among the return emigrants engaged in agriculture and allied activities in the post-return phase, only 62 per cent had worked in this sector prior to emigration. Ten per cent had moved from construction, 10 per cent from other services and 9 per cent from trade and commerce. While 8 per cent of those employed in agriculture had moved to construction, 10 per cent had moved from construction to agriculture. Nearly 38 per cent of workers in agriculture (after return) had moved to this field from other sectors. Similarly, around 53 per cent of workers in manufacturing had not worked in this sector before emigration: agriculture contributed 12.2 per cent, trade and commerce 10.2 per cent and other services 10.2 per cent. In the post-return phase, workers in trade and commerce included of 11.8 per cent from agriculture, 8 per cent each from construction, transport and other services. Thus, emigration and return emigration contributed considerably to the redistribution of workers by industrial categories.

If all the sectors are taken together, only 57 per cent of return emigrants were engaged in their original sectors. The remaining 43 per cent were engaged in activities other than the one they had pursued before emigration. The overall index of sector mobility was 43 per cent (Table 5.16).

TABLE 5.16: PER CENT OF RETURN EMIGRANTS WHO CHANGED/UNCHANGED INDUSTRY SECTOR BEFORE EMIGRATION AND AFTER RETURN

	Unchanged (%)	*Changed (%)*
Agriculture	68.9	31.1
Manufacturing	54.8	45.2
Trade. Commerce	60.3	39.7
Transport	72.9	27.1
Construction	62.1	37.9
Services	34.6	65.4
All	57.4	43.6

Source: Field survey, 2001.

Thus, there was a significant change in the industrial classification of workers because of emigration and return. The highest mobility was among workers in other services: 65.4 per cent (Figure 5.2). This was followed by manufacturing (45.2), trade and commerce (39.7), construction (37.9), agriculture (31.1) and transport (27.1). Transport was one sector which retained most of its workers (72.9 per cent).

Overall, the transition in the economic activity of return

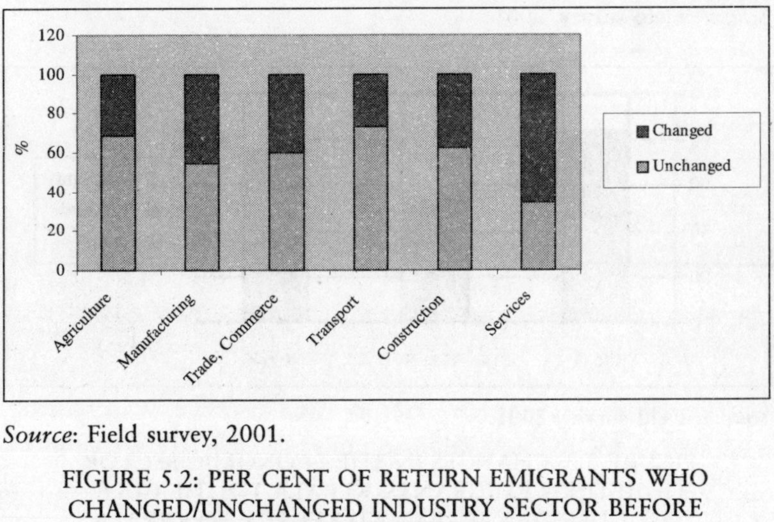

Source: Field survey, 2001.

FIGURE 5.2: PER CENT OF RETURN EMIGRANTS WHO CHANGED/UNCHANGED INDUSTRY SECTOR BEFORE EMIGRATION AND AFTER RETURN

emigrants between employment prior to emigration and employment in the foreign country (53.7 per cent) was smaller than that between employment in the foreign country and employment in Kerala in the post-return phase (64.8 per cent). The least change in activity was between before emigration and after return (43 per cent) (Table 5.17 and Figure 5.3).

Among the workers in agriculture in the post-return phase, only 61.5 per cent had worked in that sector prior to emigration. Ten per cent were in construction. Around 38.5 per cent of return

TABLE 5.17: PER CENT WHO REMAINED IN THE SAME INDUSTRY BEFORE EMIGRATION AND AFTER RETURN

Sector	%
Agriculture Animal Husbandry	68.9
Mining/Quarrying	0.0
Manufacturing	54.8
Construction	62.1
Trade, Commerce, Hotels	60.3
Transport	72.9
Other Services	34.6
Others	22.2
Total	54.0

Source: Field survey, 2001.

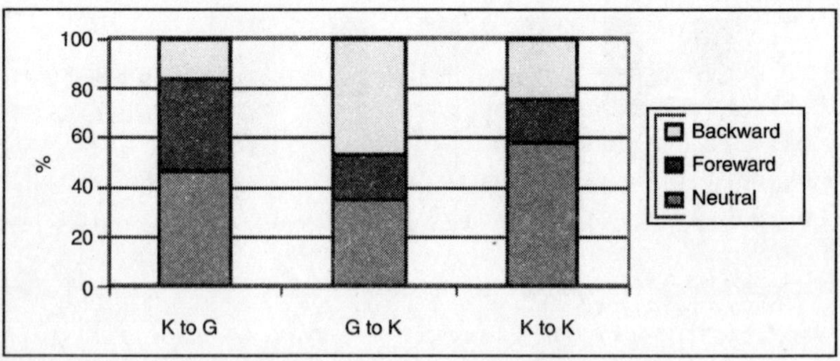

Source: Field survey, 2001.

FIGURE 5.3: CHANGES IN THE ECONOMIC SECTOR OF RETURN EMIGRANTS: KERALA TO THE GULF, THE GULF TO KERALA AND KERALA TO KERALA

emigrants in agriculture had shifted to agriculture from other sectors. Similarly, 53.1 per cent of workers in manufacturing were not engaged in this sector prior to emigration. The changes in the other sectors are given in Table 5.18.

TABLE 5.18: PER CENT OF WORKERS IN A SECTOR WHO MOVED TO IT AFTER RETURN TO KERALA

Sector	%
Agriculture Animal Husbandry	38.5
Mining/Quarrying	10.0
Manufacturing	53.1
Construction	25.8
Trade, Commerce, Hotels	48.5
Transport	42.7
Other Services	41.8
Others	72.4

Source: Field survey, 2001.

The change in economic activity of return emigrants as between pre-emigration and stay abroad was larger than that between pre-emigration and post-return.

It has often been postulated that economic growth has been, historically speaking, marked by shifts in the industrial distribution of workers—first from the primary to the secondary sector and then from the secondary to the tertiary sector. The extent to which the changes observed in the industrial classification of return emigrants between the pre-emigration and post-return phases was indicative of economic growth in Kerala was not obvious. The fact that a large number of persons who had worked in the secondary and tertiary sectors in the Gulf countries had moved to the primary sector and that the proportion who were employed in manufacturing—related activities were few indicated that Kerala continues to be an agrarian, pre-industrial economy.

CHAPTER 6

Problems of Emigration

Return emigration is the final phase of the emigration process. Thus, problems of return emigrants begin with difficulties related to preparation for emigration, much before emigration from Kerala really takes place. The different phases and facets of the process of emigration and the problems associated with it are discussed here.

PRE-EMIGRATION PHASE

The decision to emigrate was influenced by the socio-economic conditions at home as compared to those in the prospective destinations. In this respect, conditions in Kerala are ideal for emigration. Not only is the density of population in the state one of the highest in India, but also unemployment rate, particularly among the educated, is the highest for any state in India. What is needed for massive emigration is the demand for their services. This demand was created on a large scale in the Gulf countries with the oil boom of 1973-4.

As expected, over 70 per cent of return emigrants reported that the basic reason for emigration was lack of employment opportunities in Kerala. This was followed by the desire to improve living standards over 60 per cent. Other reasons mentioned by return emigrants were discharge of family responsibilities and redemption of family debts. Thus, the reasons for emigration were basically economic in nature: to get jobs, to earn money and to improve living standards (Table 6.1).

The people of Kerala are by nature home-bound. They prefer to work in their home surroundings. However, when income levels are low, aspirations are high and opportunities are remote people are constrained to look for opportunities elsewhere. In Kerala, opportunities for earning an adequate income have

TABLE 6.1: REASONS FOR EMIGRATION

	First	*Second*	*Third*
Lack of Employment in Kerala	275	38	26
To Improve Living Standard	34	235	35
To Redeem Debts	32	36	105
Discharge Family Responsibilities	15	26	142
To Accumulate Fund for Investments	10	31	49
For Pleasure of Travelling	11	1	12
Others	3	11	–

Source: Field survey, 2001.

dwindled steadily over the past several decades. Unemployment has increased both in absolute and relative terms. Thus, the lack of job opportunities, lack of scope for improving their living standards and non-existence of sources for discharging their family responsibilities and redeeming their families from indebtedness compel people to outmigrate or emigrate. It is not surprising that when opportunities for employment opened up in the Middle East they rushed to grab them.

Source of Information

Emigration requires information about employment opportunities and conditions of work abroad. The major sources of information for the respondents are presented in Table 6.2. The most important source cited by 55.2 per cent of the respondents was friends and relatives. Next in importance was recruiting agencies which was mentioned by nearly two-fifths of return emigrants. Surprisingly, news media and emigrants on home visits were not important sources.

Information about emigration prospects is not sufficient for emigrating. The prospective emigrant should be assured of a job

TABLE 6.2: SOURCE OF INFORMATION ABOUT EMIGRATION

Source	*% Who Got Information from*
Friends and Relatives	55.2
Recruiting Agencies	38.1
News Media	5.1
Emigrants on Home Visits	1.6

Sources: Field survey, 2001.

either before emigration or on arrival at the destination. In this case too, it was mainly help from friends, relatives and recruiting agents that enabled them to secure a job abroad. Four out of ten respondents got their first job through the help of friends and relatives, one-fourth with the assistance of licensed recruiting agents and 15 per cent through unlicensed recruiting agents. Government agencies played a minor role in this (Table 6.3).

TABLE 6.3: AGENCIES THROUGH WHICH FIRST EMPLOYMENT WAS SECURED

Friends and Relatives	41.1
Through Licensed Recruiting Agencies	23.9
Through Unlicensed Recruiting Agencies	15.3
Direct Application	10.2
Through Other Contacts	3.0
Through Government Agencies	2.4
Through Pilgrimage	1.6
By Means of Visiting Visas	1.3
Through Construction Firms	0.5
Other Means	0.7
Total	100.0

Source: Field survey, 2001.

Nearly half of the return emigrants had entered into formal contracts for employment before they proceeded to the Gulf countries, and 7 per cent had received formal letters of consent from their prospective employers offering them jobs on reaching their destination. Thus, around 55 per cent of the emigrants had some secure contract before they emigrated. As for the remaining 45 per cent, they had no such assurance, in their case it was a leap in the dark (see Table 6.4).

TABLE 6.4: TYPES OF CONTRACT FOR EMPLOYMENT ABROAD

Formal Contract	47.8
Letter from Employer	7.1
No Formal Contract	44.3
Others	0.7
Total	100.0

Source: Field survey, 2001.

Contracts were written either in English (54 per cent) or in Arabic (44 per cent). Nearly 57 per cent had received some pre-emigration counsel about conditions of employment abroad mostly from friends (59 per cent) and relatives (41 per cent). This advice proved to be invaluable for the emigrants.

COST OF EMIGRATION

A major problem facing the prospective emigrants was finances to meet the costs of emigration. Emigration from Kerala is by no means a low cost proposition. On an average, an emigrant had to arrange Rs. 33,000 for meeting the various expenses incurred in connection with emigration.

The major visa (Rs. 21,000), air travel (Rs. 11,000) and payment to recruiting agencies (Rs. 8,900) and other intermediaries (Rs. 6,100). An additional cost was borne by about 5 per cent of the respondents because they were duped by one agency another dealing with recruitment, emigration clearance or air travel. The amount lost on this account was Rs. 12,000 per emigrant. Expenses incurred on obtaining passports and getting emigration clearance were relatively small (Table 6.5).

TABLE 6.5: COST OF EMIGRATION

	Average Cost (Rs.)
Payment to Recruiting Agents	8,890
Payment to Other Intermediaries	6,151
Passport	681
Visa	21,203
Air Ticket	10,968
Emigration Clearance	1,988
Loss Due to Fraud	12,097
Total Average Cost	33,003

Source: Field survey, 2001.

Most of the emigrants to the Middle East came from relatively poor households who could ill-afford to spend around Rs. 33,000 from their own resources. Nearly 60 per cent of them had to resort to borrowing; loans were raised from friends and relatives, moneylenders and banking institutions. A few even resorted to the sale or mortgage of landed assets, financial assets or ornaments and jewellery. Government's assistance in this matter was insignificant. This is an area where the government and the banks should have played a larger role (Table 6.6).

TABLE 6.6: PER CENT OF RETURN EMIGRANTS WHO MET THE COST OF EMIGRATION FROM VARIOUS SOURCES

Source of Financing	%
Personal Savings	28.6
Parents Savings	20.1
Borrowing	59.5
Loans, Moneylenders	14.7
Loans, Banks	5.2
Sale/Mortgage Land	10.1
Sale/Pledge Financial Assets	4.5
Sale/Pledge Ornaments	36.2
Government Assistance	1.2
Others	5.4

Sources: Field survey, 2001.
Note: Figures do not add up to 100 since several return emigrants had more than one source of financing.

Problems at Destination

Problems faced by the respondents in the Gulf countries, from the time they disembarked to the time of their return home, were minimal (see Table 6.7). The general impression among the public in Kerala is that emigrants have a difficult time in the Gulf countries. There are innumerable stories about forged visas, fake job contracts, arrests and imprisonment on disembarking at airports in the Gulf, long hours of hard work under unhealthy conditions, denial of permission to keep their passports, denial of the right to change jobs, inability to return home for lack of means or inability to retrieve their passports. These stories are counterbalanced by numerous instances of emigrants making huge remittances, returning home with a variety of luxury goods, constructing huge mansions, sending children to prestigious and expensive schools, and providing parents and other family members the best possible medical treatment.

TABLE 6.7: PROBLEMS AND ISSUES ENCOUNTERED IN THE GULF COUNTRIES

	%
Problems with	
Passport	0.6
Visa	2.3
Work Permit	4.3
Contact on Arrival	
Employers Representative	36.2
Friends/Relatives	61.0
Indian Embassy	1.4
None	1.4
Received the Same Employment as Promised	
Yes	66.9
No	33.1
Type of Treatment Received in the Gulf Compared with that Received by Other Nationals	
More Favourable	23.4
Same as that for Other Nationalities	49.9
Not the same as for Other Nationals	26.7
Whether Signed a Second Contract?	
Yes	24.4
No	75.6
Whether Allowed to Keep Your Passport?	
Yes	11.6
No	88.4
Housing Accommodation	
Good	22.5
Adequate	68.5
Poor	8.9
Shared Housing Accommodation with Others?	
Yes	13.8
No	86.2
Quality of Food	
Excellent	11.3
Good	82.0
Poor	6.7

(Contd.)

Was Food Free of Cost?	
Free	16.4
Subsidized	13.7
Market Value	69.9
How was the Medical Care?	
Good	20.3
Satisfactory	61.3
Poor	10.5
No Facilities	7.9
How were the Educational Facilities?	
Good	34.1
Satisfactory	41.8
Poor	11.9
No Facilities	12.2
Were there Adequate Facilities for Religious Observance?	
Yes	71.4
No	28.6
Did your Wife Live with You?	
Yes	11.5
No	88.5
Was the Spouse Employed?	
Yes	55.2
No	44.8
Reasons for not Bringing Wife	
Lack of Accommodation	5.2
Insufficient Income	79.0
Desire to Maximize Income	7.3
Difficult to get Job for Wife	1.8
Spouse Employed at Home	2.6
Restriction at Host Country	0.4
Permission Denied by India	0.0
Education of Children	1.8
Unwillingness of Spouse	1.9
Did you Seek Assistance from the Indian Consulate?	
Yes	9.4
No	90.4
What Sort of Assistance?	
Grievance with Employer	20.0

(Contd.)

Problems Related to Remittance	11.0
Communication problems with Home	5.0
Legal problems in Host Country	17.0
Others	47.0
Were you Satisfied with the Assistance?	
Yes	65.9
No	34.1

What did the return emigrants think about their living and working conditions abroad? Very few of the respondents of the present survey had encountered any major problem when they arrived in the Gulf. Less than 1 per cent had problems with passports; below 3 per cent with visas and less than 5 per cent with work permits.

On arrival in the Gulf, most of them were received by friends or relatives. Employers' representatives were there to receive one-third of them. In very few cases neither the employers' representatives nor friends or relatives or even an official of the Indian embassy came to receive them.

Two-thirds of return emigrants were assigned jobs that had been promised to them. Three-fourths reported that they received the expected or even better treatment from their employers. In fact, some believed that they were given even better treatment than expatriate workers from other Asian countries. Around one-fourth had to sign a second contract, but three-fourths did not have to do so.

An overwhelming 88 per cent of return emigrants were not allowed to keep their passports. This was the most glaring violation of freedom the emigrants experienced in the Gulf countries.

Over 80 per cent were of the opinion that the housing provided to them was adequate or good and only 14 per cent had to share accommodation with friends. There were no complaints about the quality of food. Over 90 per cent reported that the food was good or excellent. Only a small proportion was provided food free of cost. Around 70 per cent bought food at the prevailing prices but 14 per cent got it at subsidized prices. The type of medical care provided in the Gulf countries was described as good by about one-fifth and satisfactory by more than three-fifths of the respondents. Similarly, the educational facilities for their children were described as good by about one-third and as satisfactory by over two-fifths of return emigrants. Facilities were available for religious observances as well. However, about one-fourth of return emigrants were of the opinion that facilities for practising their religion (other than Islam) could have been better.

Less than 10 per cent of the respondents were accompanied by their wives. In half of such cases, the wives were employed. Low income was the main reason cited by the majority for not being able to take their wives to the Gulf. Only 5 per cent mentioned lack of accommodation as the reason.

Nearly 10 per cent of the respondents mentioned that they had sought help from the Indian embassy in the Gulf; the remaining 90 per cent did not approach the embassy during their entire sojourn abroad. Assistance from the embassy was sought to settle disputes with employers or for resolving legal problems. Those who had sought assistance were largely satisfied with the services they had received.

COST AND BENEFIT OF THE EMIGRATION EXPERIENCE

The per capita average monthly income of return emigrants in the Gulf countries was Rs. 10,113; their per capita average monthly expenses were only Rs. 3,574. On an average, an emigrant saved Rs. 6,539. Out of savings, as emigrant remitted home Rs. 3,517 per month.

Nearly 90 per cent of the respondents had made remittances on a regular basis either to their spouses or, in very few cases, to their parents or other immediate relatives. Banks were the principal channel through which remittances were made (Table 6.8).

One hears of many cases of emigrants being cheated when they sent money home; but the respondents reported very few cases of cheating. They were duped, strangely enough, not by strangers, agencies or organizations (such as banks), but by their friends, relatives or immediate neighbours.

TABLE 6.8: ISSUES RELATED TO RETURN EMIGRANTS

Responsibility for Managing Migrants Household Back Home		
Spouse		39.8
Migrant's Parents		53.9
Parents of Spouse		2.4
Others		3.9
Did you Send any Remittances Home?		
Yes		90.2
No		9.7
To Whom did You Make Remittances?		
Spouse		33.3*
Migrant's Parents		36.6
Spouse's Parents		0.7
Others		4.0
Channel for Remittances		
Through Friends		4.6*
Banks		54.9
Mail Transfer		0.7
NRI Deposit		16.9
Any Instance of Getting Cheated?		
Yes		2.2
No		97.8
Agency which Cheated		
Friends/Relatives/Neighbours		63.6
Non-banking Financial Institutions		18.2
Banks		18.2
Any Bank Account?	*Now*	*Before Emigration*
Current Account	17.7	7.9
Savings Account	36.4	17.1
Fixed Deposit	10.6	2.9
Family Problems When You were Away?		
Illness in the Family		16.5
Death		13.3
Loss of Assets		1.3
Threats to Personal Safety		0.9
Disputes		0.6

Note: * Percentages do not add up to 100 as in some cases more than one person received the remittances.

Sources: Field survey, 2001.

THREAT OF LOSS OF JOB

The number of return migrants who came back home in recent years was far more than the number in the earlier years. The number of persons who returned during 1996-2000 was 1.7 times the number who had returned during 1991-5.

With much higher earnings in the Gulf compared to earnings in Kerala, why did so many emigrants return? There are several reasons (see Table 6.9). In two-fifths of the cases, the period of their contract had expired or their employers had terminated their jobs. The next important reason was difficult working conditions abroad. More than one-fifth of return emigrants came back because they could no longer tolerate the difficult working conditions. They had been accustomed to easy working conditions in Kerala. Difficult living conditions, particularly extremes of temperature, for example, were unbearable for them and more so in the case of those whose health was poor. Due to ill health, injury and accidents one-eighth of the respondents were forced to return home. Exigencies at home forced one-eighth of them to return (Table 6.9).

Thus, the major reasons for returning were expiry of the contract or repatriation. There is not much scope in any of the

TABLE 6.9: REASONS FOR RETURN

Due to	%
Expiry of Contract	30.3
Resigned due to Difficult Living Conditions	12.9
Resigned due to Difficult Working Conditions	22.9
Job Terminated by Employer	10.3
Political Upheaval	1.9
Illegal Stay Abroad Compulsory Repatriation	5.4
Condition at Home Required Presence	13.7
Ill-health	11.1
Injury/Accident/ Incapacitation	1.2
	100.0

Note: Percentages do not add up to 100, as in several cases, there was more than one reason for return.

Sources: Field survey, 2001.

Gulf countries for appeal against an employer's decision to terminate the services of an expatriate worker. There are no labour laws in these countries. Delayed payment of salaries, arbitrary deduction of salaries by employers and abolition of non-wage benefits were some of the other reasons for return cited by the respondents.

CHAPTER 7

Rehabilitation and Development

REHABILITATION OF RETURN EMIGRANTS

Two questions that are uppermost in the minds of return emigrants and government officials dealing with emigration problems are rehabilitation of return emigrants and the ways in which their expertise and capital assets could be utilized for developmental activities in Kerala. These are not separate questions. If the return emigrants' skills and capital could be used for the development of the state, then this process could automatically lead to the rehabilitation of a majority of them. However, a small proportion of return emigrants would not be covered by such an approach; they would require special help through social security and welfare programmes (Prakash, 1998; Irudaya Rajan, 2004; Zachariah, Kannan and Irudaya Rajan, 2002).

First we will discuss the demands raised by various associations of return emigrants and then examine the policies and policy pronouncements of the state government for their welfare and rehabilitation. The results of the field enquiry with respect to this question are presented, followed by the policy recommendations that emerge from the discussion.

ASSOCIATIONS OF RETURN EMIGRANTS AND THEIR DEMANDS

At present, there are hundreds of associations of return emigrants; most of them were established during the past three years (Appendix III). A couple of associations were set up towards the end of the 1980s, but they remained near-dormant till about 1998. The mushrooming of returnee associations since 1997 seems to have been due largely to the formation of the separate department of the state government specifically for the purpose of looking into the problems of non-resident Keralites.

Even though there are a large number of associations of returnee emigrants, most of them exist only in name. The activities of the associations have been confined till date to submission of occasional petitions and memoranda of demands to governments at the state and at the centre outlining the requirements of return emigrants in relation to welfare, rehabilitation and development.

In order to ascertain the nature of activities of these associations, we made repeated attempts to interview them. The response rate was very poor and, not unexpectedly, a large number of invitations that were sent by mail, came back with the endorsement 'addressee not found'. On the basis of a few interviews (with representatives of about half a dozen associations) and examination of a large number of memoranda received by NORKA and NORKWA, it is clear that their demands fall under three categories: welfare, rehabilitation and development.

The specific demands under these three categories are as follows:

Welfare

1. Special educational facilities and educational concessions for children of return emigrants.
2. Free medical treatment for poor returnees.
3. Minimum monthly pension of Rs. 150 to all returnees above 55 years of age.
4. Insurance for the returnees and their dependents.
5. Employment for dependents of deceased emigrants.
6. Compensation for losses incurred due to breach of contract by foreign sponsors or employers.

Rehabilitation

1. Interest-free housing schemes.
2. Job reservation in central and state governments and other public sector organizations.
3. Loan facilities at concessional rates of interest for self-employment schemes.
4. Age exemption for appointment to government jobs.

5. Creation of posts specifically for the employment of returned emigrants.
6. Training/apprenticeship in public sector undertakings for returnees.
7. Job reservation for poor female returned emigrants, in government and other public sector undertakings such as the Civil Supplies Corporation.
8. Extending the coverage of the IRDP and other programmes for the poor to poor female returnee emigrants.
9. Grant of licence to run foreign liquor and toddy shops.
10. Reinstatement of returnee emigrants to jobs held by them prior to emigration after condoning break of service, non-reporting for job in time, etc.
11. Preference in granting of licence to run restaurants, vehicle parks, communication centres, etc.
12. Creation of a growth fund (by mobilizing long-term deposits offering rates of interest higher than the market rate) from NRKs for starting enterprises for employment of returnees.

DEVELOPMENT

1. Industrial investment by government specifically for returnees.
2. Bank credit to returnees for investment, at low rates of interest.
3. Bank exclusively for returnees.
4. Condonement of default on the part of returnees in repayment of bank loans.
5. Leasing out of uncultivated land for agricultural purposes to organizations of returnees.
6. Preference to returnees in tourism development schemes.
7. Loans up to Rs. 25,000 to returnees without collateral.
8. Entrusting of public sector undertakings incurring losses to groups of return emigrants.

Apart from these demands, there are a few others of a very general nature such as:

1. Creation of a climate conducive to investment in the state.

2. Prevention of harassment of enterprises of returnees by the bureaucracy and political parties.
3. Formation of panchayat level labour contract societies of return migrants.
4. Banning of *bandhs*, strikes and *jathas*.

The associations have also demanded the refund of the emigration deposits collected from emigrants at the time of emigration clearance. As has been mentioned earlier, none of the associations has undertaken any activity of its own other than the submission of memoranda of demands. Nor do they have specific information about the magnitude and categories of return emigrants who need social security support, rehabilitation assistance and developmental guidance and protection, respectively.

State Government Policies on Rehabilitation of Return Migrants

The phenomenon of return migration from the Gulf countries was not included in discussions on emigration in Kerala till about the dawn of the 1980s. A study in 1983 noted for the first time that the return of emigrants was likely to accelerate because the peak period of construction activities was coming to an end in the Gulf countries. The government of Kerala was not oblivious to the impending possibility of massive return of emigrants and the problem of their rehabilitation. As early as May 1983, the Minister of state for Industries announced that the government was considering a plan to establish industrial estates in different parts of Kerala to provide employment to repatriates. He added that 100 electronics industry units would be set up of which one-third would be reserved for Gulf repatriates. He also spoke of starting television assembly units in selected emigration pockets in the state (Nair, 1986). In 1984, the Kerala government announced that an investment company was being formed for mobilizing funds from Keralites in the Middle East and investing them in industrial ventures in the state. This was followed by a declaration in 1986 that the state would set up small scale and medium industries to provide employment to emigrants returning from the Gulf countries (Nair, 1989; Zachariah and Irudaya Rajan, 2004).

The attention of the Government of India was drawn to the problem of rehabilitation of return emigrants only in 1994 when it issued directions to state governments to form societies to guide and assist return emigrants' rehabilitation through self-employment, skill upgradation and wage employment. Employment exchanges were instructed by the central government to maintain separate registers of return migrants and render them requisite assistance for placement in jobs (Nair, 1999). However, all these declarations, pronouncements and instructions of both the state and central governments have remained on paper till date.

In 1996, the Kerala government took the initiative to adopt a series of positive measures to look into the problems of emigrants in the special context of the repatriation of several thousands of 'amnesty returnees' from the UAE. However, these measures were not disigned exclusively for return emigrants, but for all emigrants from Kerala in all foreign countries and outmigrants in the other states of India and at all the stages in the process of migration. In August 1996, the government decided to set up a separate department, NORKA, to look into the problems of non-resident Keralites.

The major areas of concern of this department were welfare of emigrants and outmigrants and investment facilitation for them. The issues included under welfare were problems relating to visa, accidents or deaths and grievances of non-resident Keralites as well as their families back home. Under investment facilitation, the major focus was on the channelization of remittances of non-resident Keralites into productive sectors in the state. Rehabilitation figured in the scheme as a major item and referred to provisions for placement in jobs, or assistance in self-employment, of emigrants who returned without adequate means of livelihood. The proposed department, Non-Resident Keralites' Affairs (NORKA), was set up in December 1996.

In May 1997 NORKA introduced an accident and death insurance scheme for non-resident Keralites. The membership of this scheme has been steadily increasing and was around

1.78 lakh at the end of December 2001. The activities of NORKA were planned to be diversified and a subsidiary unit, Non-Resident Keralites Welfare Agency (NORKWA), was established by the end of 2000. Till the end of November 2001, insurance benefits under this scheme were given in eighteen cases. NORWKA was intended to be an agency for planning and implementation of schemes for the welfare of Keralites residing abroad and setting up of or assisting in joint ventures with them. Some of the activities proposed for addressing welfare problems which emigrants could encounter after return or repatriation, included the following:

1. Pension scheme to be introduced based on a fund raised by contributions from non-resident Keralites working abroad and the government of Kerala.
2. Social security scheme which would provide insurance coverage in the event of death or permanent disability caused by an accident abroad.
3. Medical insurance scheme for the medical treatment of return emigrants and their families.

The other subsidiaries proposed to be introduced under NORKWA include *Pravasi* (Non-resident) welfare fund, NRK investment bank, satellite township (called NRK Heritage Home), NORKWA shipping corporation and *Pravasi Suraksha* (Non-resident Security), *Kudumba Arogya* (Family Health) and *Pravasi Vanitha Suraksha* (Non-resident Women's Security) schemes. NORKA has constituted a Non-Resident Keralite Infrastructure Initiative Fund with a view to financing joint public–private infrastructure projects in the state.

At a state level convention held on 18 December 2001 at Thiruvananthapuram, attended by several State Ministers including the Chief Minister, the government announced its intention to adopt a series of measures for the welfare and rehabilitation of return emigrants. The proposed measures included the following:

1. Formation of a databank of emigrants and return emigrants.
2. Establishment of a welfare corporation for NRKs.
3. Assistance and counselling to return emigrants to launch self-employment projects.

4. Creation of an accident insurance board.
5. Refund of emigration fee to return emigrants.
6. Exempt of import duty to bring tools and equipment worth up to Rs. 10,000,00 for setting up enterprises.
7. Educational assistance to children of NRKs and return emigrants.

The Non-Residents Keralites Welfare Agency was renamed ROOTS NRK Development Initiative in 2001 and registered under Section 25 of the Indian Companies Act, 1956. The main objective of ROOTS is the welfare, rehabilitation and development of return emigrants from all over the world through investment programmes for them. Its specific objectives are:

1. To plan and implement programmes and schemes for the welfare and benefit of non-resident Keralites and to address and devise solutions to their problems.
2. To provide every assistance to NRKs and to take up matters concerning them with the state and central governments and other institutions and organizations in India and abroad.
3. To evolve strategies for the resettlement and reintegration of NRKs returning to Kerala and to other Indian states.
4. To give a thrust to the industrial development of the state by channelizing the NRKs' resources and expertise and helping them to set up projects, ventures and enterprises in Kerala.
5. To facilitate the creation of a high calibre human resource pool to meet the changing global requirements and to assist and monitor human resources export through transparent and lawful methods.
6. To undertake the establishment, management and monitoring of a worldwide network of organizations and groups of NRKs.

ROOTS envisages a large number of welfare, financial, entrepreneurial, research and other activities for NRKs. Welfare activities include the following:

1. *A pension scheme for all NRKs* called *Pravasi Swasraya*, a social security scheme that ensures regular monthly income to NRKs as and when they return. Various schemes offering

medical/accident insurance, free medical check-ups, and associated benefits.

2. *Insurance schemes and a welfare fund for returnees*, a comprehensive welfare package has been designed to suit the requirements of all return migrants. *Suvidha*, a welfare fund which would help in the reintegration of the returnee migrants, is under purview.
3. *An extreme contingent repatriation scheme* is testimony to the government's concern for the repatriation of stranded persons and those injured and to bring back the mortal remains of persons dying abroad.

Among the financial and entrepreneurial activities envisaged are *an entrepreneurship development programme* which adopts a concerted approach to attract and encourage investment in the state. The programme covers consultancy, counselling, project initiative fund and institutional linkage for finance; and *a growth fund* of Rs. 200 crore to 500 crore to finance major institutional infrastructural projects in the state.

Planning and research activities of ROOTS include the preparation and maintenance of a data bank of NRKs spread across the world; undertaking a migration monitoring study in the three international airports, to provide inputs for long-term planning and policy formulation; and the implementation of a skill upgradation course conducted by a panel of top resources personnel and establishment of centres of excellence.

The other projects included under Roots are heritage homes (in the southern districts of Kerala); shipping service between Kochi and the Gulf region; and interactions with returnee associations.

Three types of annual conventions are planned to be held at the government's initiative: *Samavayam* focusing on the issues of Malayalis working abroad, *Samanwayam* targeting Malayalis residing in other states in India, and *Samaganam*, a forum for return migrants.

NORKA claims to have taken up several types of services to solve the problems faced by non-resident Keralites working abroad. These services, rendered in liaison with various official agencies, include:

- *Along with the Indian embassies* verification of the bona-fides of work visas; tracing Keralites reported to be missing abroad and bringing them back to Kerala; securing the release of Keralites undergoing prison sentences because of false legal suits against them; freeing persons illegally detained by sponsors, employers and touts; sending back Keralites who have lost their jobs; offering solace to victims of accidents; sending the mortal remains of Malayalis dying abroad to Kerala without delay and offering legal solutions to labour disputes.
- *Coordinating with the Passport Offices* to ensure that emigrants are issued new passports or their old passports are renewed promptly in an emergency; rendering legal assistance to those who have lost their passports or whose passports have been cancelled because of their illegal activities such as having more than one passport or having passports in false names and addresses, and to issue passports to those who find it impossible to avail or accept foreign jobs for want of passport.
- *Seeking the assistance of the Revenue and Home Departments* to redress allegations or complaints against migrants' families relating to border disputes, the use of lanes or pathways, encroachment on land and other immovable properties on the basis of forged legal documents, harassment of elderly persons, women and children living alone in households, harassment of women, charging a fee for bogus visas, and betrayal of clients on the basis of records of bogus transactions.
- *Eliciting the involvement of the electricity board and telecom authorities* to draw attention to complaints regarding excessive telephone/electricity bills, unauthorized wire/cable lines stretched over habitats, delays in replacing damaged meters/telephone receivers, wires/cables obstructing vehicular traffic, etc.
- *Coordinating with the airport customs* to look into and resolve issues pertaining to harassment, theft of passengers' baggage and levy of grossly excessive duties on baggage, etc., by customs officers at the airports.

- *Contacting the flight services* to address complaints regarding loss or theft of luggage, levy of excessive flight and freight charges and loss of jobs due to cancellation of flights at the last moment.
- *Involving the local government* to look into inordinate delays in granting permission for construction of buildings, anomalies in the building tax imposed, construction of roads through the landed properties of migrants and problems relating to the issue of birth and death certificates and similar negation of civil rights.
- *Coordinating with the Health Department* to solve the problems of migrants pertaining to medical certificates, denial of service benefits, and difficulties in getting leave of absence for long periods.
- *Seeking the assistance of the Education Department* to issue new education certificates to migrants who have lost their education certificates without any delay and to redress complaints of denial of service benefits, etc.
- *Coordinating with the Transport Department* help solve to migrants' problems of obtaining a driving license, vehicle permits and vehicle tax.
- *Liaisoning with the Post/Telegraph Department* to redress migrants' complaints of theft or loss of parcels and letters and unwarranted delay in the delivery of parcels, letters and other communications.

The complaints received by the Chief Minister, the NORKA Minister, Secretary of the NORKA Department and others, pertaining to matters already discussed here, are dealt with appropriately depending on the importance and urgency of each, through facsimile, e-mail and even on the telephone, and remedies and solutions are offered promptly.

The Chief Minister along with the NORKA Minister periodically bring to the notice of the Prime Minister petitions received from migrants against frequent upward revision of air fare by Air India, reducing the sentence periods in the Gulf countries, inclusion of migrants' names in the electoral list, ensuring that the mortal remains of migrants who die in foreign countries are sent home gratis, simplification of the Hindi syllabus for the benefit of CBSE students of the Gulf countries, etc.

Memoranda containing the demands of migrants have been submitted by the NOKKA Minister to the central ministry of civil aviation. These demands include checking the practice of airline companies to like air fares frequently and cancel flights arbitrarily, solution to the problems of theft and loss of luggage, issuing instructions to Air India to introduce more flights to Kerala during the festival season, granting international status to the Kozhikode airport, setting up additional terminals in the Thiruvananthapuram airport, permitting free travel to one person who would bring the mortal remains of persons dying abroad to Kerala. Similar memoranda have been submitted to the central ministries of External Affairs, Labour and Surface Transport.

A centre for attestation of educational certificates of prospective migrants to the UAE was set up at Vazhuthakad in Thiruvananthapuram under the auspices of ROOTS in January 2004. There are facilities for online registration as well. ROOTS has provided facilities for getting the attested certificates of job seekers re-attested by the central Ministries of Human Resources and External Affairs and the Embassy of the UAE.

Programmes for local development such as 'My Village, My Dream' and 'My Malayalam, My Pride' are to be implemented with migrants' efforts either individually or through team effort. Besides, 'Heritage Homes' for the aged parents of migrants, shipping services from Kochi to the Gulf countries, establishment of a NORKA cell in Delhi to laision with the central ministries of External Affairs and Home, and diplomatic offices of other countries located in Delhi, establishment of a state level monitoring committee against bogus recruitment are being implemented. In addition, disaster cells established under the auspices of NORKA at Delhi and Thiruvananthapuram have earned the accolade of the media and social workers. All the welfare programmes of NORKA are implemented by ROOTS.

For the welfare and rehabilitation of return migrants living below the poverty line, a welfare fund, *Santhwana*, has been set up. The beneficiaries are those who lost their jobs as domestic help, plantation workers and construction workers and were repatriated. *Santhwana* is envisaged to help these hapless people.

Pravasi Swasraya serves as the corporate agent of the LIC. A Total Insurance Solution Package (TISP) is also in the offing. This offers a bouquet of different insurance schemes suited to various income groups. It comprises health insurance, accident insurance, pension schemes, Janashree Bima Yojana for low income groups, Universal Health Insurance, and Pravasi Bharatiya Bima Health Insurance, which has been mandatory for persons going abroad for the first time.

The Emergency Repatriation Fund focuses on the safe return of those who were rejected by sponsors and who were victims of accidents and to ensure that the bodies of poor people are sent home.

The Legal Assistance Cell, which has been one of the long standing demands of migrant *Malayalis*, has become operational. The bulk of complaints received by the department pertain to harassment and exploitation of migrants in their work places abroad and to trying circumstances faced by their families in Kerala. The major drawback of the families is their ignorance of their right to legal aid. The Legal Assistance Cell aims at conscientization and legal assistance.

To render legal advice to migrant Malayalis including assistance in dealing with law suits, presenting arguments in court, dealing with common legal problems, and assistance to persons who are unable to seek legal help due to economic reasons, people with expertise in criminal, civil, tax-related, and family law issues would be appointed in the Cell.

Under the overall guidance of ROOTS, it has been planned to set up small industrial units in all districts. Private companies would be established with a view to making profits. The middle income groups of migrants have evinced an interest in making investments in various industrial ventures and have been enthusiastic about rehabilitation measures. It is expected that this initiative of ROOTS would open opportunities for self-employment for migrant Keralites.

The counsel of experts on a panel formed under the programme would be available to investors who are keen to launch industrial ventures, to ensure smooth project implementation by liasing with the various government departments and to make the entrepreneurs aware of different financial institutions. Fifteen enterprises have been set up in Thiruvananthapuram and Quilon districts.

Schemes have been planned for improving the skills of prospective emigrants to the Gulf countries as well as of return migrants. These schemes aim at helping return migrants reintegrate into society as well as focus on their rehabilitation and development; and identify self-employment opportunities for migrants and their families. Applicants would receive 50 per cent fee concession. In addition, ROOTS would prepare schemes for identifying work opportunities for expatriates in foreign countries and conduct training programmes for upgradation of skills.

Plans have been made to set up a databank of expatriate Malayalis and return Malayali migrants, which would include comprehensive schemes for their welfare and rehabilitation. Steps have been taken for collecting the required information. NORKA has set up a web site www.nonresidentkeralite.com to enable the Malayali diaspora to keep in contact with one another. It has launched a bimonthly online newsletter. Facilities for online token registration of persons requiring certificate attestation have been made available on this website.

Demands Raised by Return Migrants

Most of the emigrants from Kerala belonged to poor families who went to the Gulf countries as unskilled labourers. Though their wages were higher than what they had earned prior to emigration and they had substantial savings, their tenure of service was relatively short and most of their earnings were utilized on such priorities as repaying debts, constructing houses, buying land, etc. Though they had an opulent life style initially, they found it impossible to sustain such a lifestyle once they had lost their jobs in the Middle East. Within a few years of return, many of them fell into financial difficulties and searched for any possible help including help from the government. They wanted the government's assistance is their rehabilitation and persisted in their demands.

Their main argument for government help was that while working abroad they had remitted large amounts to their state and that their remittances had helped the country to tide over the foreign exchange crises and maintain foreign exchange reserves at comfortable levels. In 2000 alone, emigrants from Kerala made remittances to the tune of Rs. 12,000 crore. Banks in Kerala had NRE deposits amounting to Rs. 13,329 crore on 31 March 1999 and Rs. 20,045 crore on 30 September 2000. The amount of NRE deposits for 2000 worked out to be more than Rs. 6,000 per capita. Return emigrants argued that in recognition of their contribution to the national foreign exchange reserves, they had a right to secure financial and other assistance from the government in their hour of need.

In the survey, we asked two questions related to the role that return emigrants expected the Kerala government to play in their rehabilitation. We asked then whether they expected the government to play any role in their rehabilitation. We had expected that all of them would give a positive response. Although an overwhelming 85 per cent did expect government support in one form or an other, about 15 per cent believed that the government did not have any role to play.

It is interesting to examine which groups expected and which did not expect any government support for rehabilitation. Among the three religious communities in the state, 83 per cent of Muslims expected government assistance while only 60 per cent of Syrian Christians had such expectations. In terms of education, the majority of return emigrants with a degree did not want help from the government while over four-fifths of those with less than the secondary level education expected government help.

The assistance expected from the government was grouped under the three categories of welfare, rehabilitation and development. Financial assistance was expected largely for development purposes such as launching business enterprises, buying automobiles and autorickshaws, setting up automobile and other workshops, establishing small-scale industries and micro enterprises for self-employment, developing agricultural land, and purchasing tools and equipment. Other purposes for which financial assistance was needed included education, medical care and marriage of children and obtaining visas for themselves or for their families to emigrate.

Pension and other welfare schemes were mentioned by about one-fourth of return emigrants while over one-fifth expected the government to provide them jobs or help them secure jobs (see Table 7.1).

An important question which arises in this context, but was not included in the field survey, was the rationale for the government to provide special financial assistance for the rehabilitation of return emigrants. In Kerala today there are 10,000,00 return outmigrants (those who came back from other states). If return emigrants are eligible for rehabilitation assistance, are return outmigrants not eligible for financial assistance for rehabilitation as well? They have also remitted large amounts to Kerala. There are around 30,000,00 educated unemployed persons who are either matriculates or have higher qualifications. Why should the government provide financial assistance or find jobs for return emigrants in preference to these educated unemployed and return outmigrants? On the same vein, why should return emigrants receive any special treatment in terms of loans for business and other productive purposes when there are many other equally or even better qualified persons in dire need of assistance?

The reason given by return emigrants as well as by return emigrants' associations is that they remitted large amounts of foreign exchange to the country. This is true and the inflow of foreign remittances is continuing as is evidenced by the large volume of NRE deposits in the banking sector of Kerala.

In our survey, we asked two questions about the income and

TABLE 7.1: TYPES OF ASSISTANCE EXPECTED FROM THE GOVERNMENT OF KERALA

Type of Assistance	%
A. Welfare	
Pensions	22.9
Other Welfare Schemes Including Medical Care	2.8
B. Rehabilitation	
Provision of Jobs or Assistance in Finding Jobs	20.3
C. Development	
Bank Loans and Government's Financial Assistance for Investment Purposes	51.8
D. Other Help in Emigration/Re-emigration	2.2
Total	100.0

Source: Field survey, 2001.

TABLE 7.2: AVERAGE MONTHLY INCOME AND EXPENSES PER RETURN EMIGRANT WHILE ABROAD

	Rs.
Average Income per Month	10,113
Average Living Expenses	3,574
Average Monthly Remittance	3,517

Source: Field survey, 2001.

expenses of return emigrants when they were working abroad.

What was your annual salary, wages or income while abroad?

What was your monthly income, what were your living expenses, what was your average home remittance?

The answer to the first question yielded an average annual income of Rs. 1,20,000 per return emigrant (see Table 7.2). The second question gave a figure of Rs. 1,21,000 as annual income. The same set of questions revealed Rs. 43,000 as the annual living expenses of each return emigrant during his/her stay abroad. The balance Rs. 77,000 was the annual saving of an emigrant. The total savings of 7,50,000 return emigrants were estimated at Rs. 5,775 crore. An average return emigrant had stayed in the Gulf for 6 years and 3 months. Thus, the accumulated savings of these return emigrants would be about Rs. 36,094 crore.

Thus, there is little doubt that return emigrants remitted huge amounts to the state. The question arises how much did the Kerala government benefit from these remittances? As noted earlier, most of the savings were spent on the construction of residential buildings, purchase of land, meeting marriage expenses and repaying debts (Table 7.3). What did the Kerala government get from return emigrants? As noted in an earlier study,

> Migration has been the single-most dynamic factor in the otherwise dreary development scenario of Kerala in the last quarter of the last century. Migration has contributed more to poverty alleviation and reduction in unemployment in Kerala than any other factor, including agrarian reforms, trade union activities and social welfare legislation (Zachariah, Mathew and Irudaya Rajan, 2003).

Through increased economic activity rendered possible by the utilization of remittances, the emigrants contributed to the increase

TABLE 7.3: USES OF SAVINGS OF RETURN EMIGRANTS

	% of Total Return Emigrants	*Average (Rs.) per Return Emigrant*
Purchase of Agricultural Land	28.7	31,102
Construction of Buildings	36.1	27,261
Marriage of Daughters, Sisters, Brothers	27.0	28,061
Higher Education	8.1	18,461
Total	100.0	56,760

Source: Field survey, 2001.

in income generation and thereby revenue collection in the state. On the basis of these arguments, return emigrants deserve greater assistance from the government in their rehabilitation.

The one public institution which has benefited most from emigration, is the banking system in the country. As noted earlier, banks in Kerala had Rs. 20,045 crore in NRE deposits in September 2000. They used these deposits for credit creation, mostly in places outside Kerala. In that process, the banking system in Kerala reaped enormous returns from the savings of emigrants from Kerala. It may be argued that the banking industry in Kerala, rather than the Kerala government, should meet the bulk of the cost of rehabilitating the unemployed return emigrants. Even assuming that they deserve help from the government, the question arises as to the type of help the government should provide. As already mentioned, return emigrants want financial assistance to set up some sort of business and also welfare assistance such as pension and concessions for medical treatment.

In this connection it is instructive to examine how and to what extent return emigrants had themselves undertaken the task of rehabilitation. In our sample of over 1,000 return emigrants, 289 had invested in some sort of self-employment. Together, they had invested Rs. 7,543,000 around or Rs. 26,100 per investor. The amount invested varied from Rs. 1,000 to 1,25,000. In 73 per cent of the cases, they had invested from their own funds. In 23 per cent of the cases, part of the funds were raised from other institutional or non-institutional sources. In only a few cases the entire capital was borrowed. More than 30 per cent of these investors had taken financial assistance from public institutions, mostly commercial banks. Very few return emigrants wanted assistance other than financial. Some of them had tried several times to launch some self-employment ventures, but had given up as their endeavours had proved to be unprofitable. The inability to identify a profit-making self-employment venture was the single most important reason for the failure of return emigrants to rehabilitate themselves.

Some of the return emigrants were unemployed at the time of our survey for a variety of reasons. It is important to examine these reasons so as to develop viable policies to rehabilitate them. Among the unemployed, 22 per cent had been previously employed for varying periods; but the remaining 88 per cent had not even attempted to find a job. Among those who had previously held jobs but had later given them up, more than half had tried to launch a project. However, they abandoned these projects as they proved to be financially unviable and loss-making ventures. Around 21 per cent had faced financial difficulties and almost 8 per cent had faced labour problems.

Further, 17 per cent of return emigrants who were not gainfully employed at the time of the survey had never even tried to set up a business venture like a store or a small-scale industry. Besides, they had never approached government agencies for assistance in starting a business. Some of them believed that they were too old to work (25 per cent) whereas others (10 per cent) were of the view that they could manage on their savings and that there was no real need to work. Around 15 per cent wanted to lead an easy life in Kerala and they did not want to be tied down by any regular work. About 40 per cent had other unspecified reasons for not working.

Return Emigrants' Potential Contribution to Kerala's Development

Return emigrants often argued that there was a vast pool of latent talent among them—technical know-how and management skills, etc.—which had remained untapped and was available for the state's development. In reality, however, this was not true for several reasons. First, the age factor was against them. Their average age was over 41 years and almost 60 per cent were above 40 years of age. Most of them were married with family responsibilities. They were not a group of dynamic young persons graduating from universities and technical schools and enthusiastically looking for challenging jobs.

Further, around 6.6 per cent of return emigrants were degree holders (i.e. a total of 50,000 in the state as a whole). The number of degree holders in a technical subject was estimated to be 2.9 per cent or around 21,000 persons. The percentage with some kind of formal technical training including certificates and diplomas was about 18.6 or 140,000 persons. Although small, there was a group of return emigrants with technical education. However, there was one problem with these numbers. Return emigrants with higher levels of education did not need any rehabilitation assistance. They wanted to be left alone to lead a peaceful life in Kerala.

A comparison of the educational levels of return emigrants with those of emigrants who had not returned reveals that the former had, on an average, lower educational levels and technical skills than the latter. Similarly, emigrants who had returned had relatively lower level jobs in the Gulf countries than those who had not returned. Those who had been self-employed in Kerala before emigration showed a higher propensity to return than those who had not been self-employed. Second, those who had been unemployed prior to emigration were less inclined to return than those who had been employed before emigration.

From the human resources point of view, return emigrants occupied a lower position than emigrants who had not returned. Most return emigrants came back for one reason or another such as loss of job, ill health or family problems. Their total human resources did not account for as much as they claimed them to be.

Return emigrants, however, had an edge over the local workers in terms of the difference in quality. On an average, a return emigrant had worked for more than 6 years in the Gulf. This gave them ample time to change their sluggish work habits and imbue a better work culture. Besides, they had learnt the meaning of an 8-hour workday. From that point of view, they would be superior to the local workers.

What material resources are at the disposal of return emigrants? Very few had any substantial financial resources as most of their. Money had been utilized for repaying debts, building houses, etc. Those who had financial resources were not interested in making any contribution to the development of the state as they wanted to lead a leisurely life.

On the basis of our findings, it may be argued that there was not much economic justification for the government to provide funds on any special concessional terms to return emigrants. It was seen that financial assistance by way of loans for small-scale industries did not cut much ice. Many of them demanded welfare assistance in terms of pensions and other benefits, but there is no justification for extending special treatment to them at the cost of the other non-migrant needy segments of the population.

Policy Recommendations

In conclusion, it may be said that there is a strong case for public assistance for rehabilitation of return emigrants. Rehabilitation of return emigrants is justifiable from the economic point of view as well as from a humanitarian perspective. The economic justification is based on the enormous contributions made by the emigrants to the social and economic development of the state in the past quarter of a century as revealed by several studies on the subject.

Return emigrants had substantial savings while they were abroad, but they had utilized most of their savings within a short time after their return. From a long-term perspective, it may be argued that the majority had mismanaged their accumulated savings, particularly in the light of the fact that they belonged to poor families. But how could they be blamed if they had invested their hard-earned money in houses, land, marriage of their dependents, and perhaps for daily subsistence at a reasonable level?

For nearly one-fifth of return emigrants, the emigration experience was a misadventure and they had lost their wealth, health and energy. There were those who had been unemployed for long periods in the Gulf countries or had trouble with the law or had fallen ill or had been involved in accidents. Their survival had become precarious and they deserve assistance on humanitarian grounds.

SUGGESTIONS

A few suggestions may be made for the rehabilitation of return emigrants who have already arrived and those who are yet to return.

1. The introduction of a welfare scheme managed by a welfare board. The scheme could include a pension scheme and an insurance scheme especially for those who have met with misfortune. An educational scheme could be planned to upgrade the skill potential of the children of return emigrants. With their newly acquired skills they could either re-emigrate or launch self-employment projects in the state.
2. The organization of cooperatives for specific tasks (e.g. public works, tourism projects) which could utilize the work discipline that the return emigrants had acquired abroad.

The seed money for all these schemes should be provided by the commercial banks of Kerala, since they have derived maximum benefit from the workers' remittances. The maintenance of the schemes on a continuing basis should be the responsibility of the emigrants (for welfare schemes and education) and return emigrants (for cooperatives).

The government may could render assistance to return emigrants who are interested in self-employment schemes or other business enterprises by way of project ideas, management training, technical advice, marketing facilities and advice to obtain bank credit or loans from other financial institutions. District level committees with the district collector as convener and representatives of ROOTS, return emigrants, banks and financial institutions, technical personnel and local level planning agencies may be useful in this matter.

There is not much justification for the government to utilize its funds on these welfare and rehabilitation efforts. However, it has an important role to play to ensure the success of these schemes. It should provide the leadership and actively assume the role of a facilitator.

CHAPTER 8

Conclusions and Recommendations

In this study, we focused attention on three aspects of the emigration process in Kerala: occupational transitions associated with emigration and return and utilization of resources—human and material—of the emigrants in the development and rehabilitation of return emigrants. The study examined the demographic, social and economic characteristics of return emigrants before emigration, after emigration to the Gulf and after return to Kerala. Further, the financial costs of and benefits of emigration, problems faced by emigrants in the Gulf countries and after return to Kerala have been discussed. A few suggestions have been made for the rehabilitation of return emigrants and their possible role in the state's development efforts.

The study revealed considerable difference between the industrial affiliation of return emigrants in Kerala before emigration and after their return to Kerala. As high as 43 per cent of return emigrants had changed their industrial sector during the period between emigration and return. However, the real transition in the economic sector, in the classical sense, that is, a systematic movement from the primary to the secondary sector and from the secondary to the tertiary sector was only about 18 per cent or less than half of the total movements. There were movements, no doubt, but very little meaningful transition. Some workers shifted from agriculture to manufacturing or service industries, whereas others moved back from manufacturing and service sectors to agriculture.

The Kerala government has hoped for assistance from emigrants and return emigrants in the state's development programmes. How much did return emigrants actually contribute? It was observed that while emigrants abroad could play a significant role in this, the role of return emigrants was limited. Kerala has three-quarters of a million return emigrants. However, the average

age of this group was 41.7 years. Some of them were too old and/ or sick to work. Others believed that there was no need for them to work as they wanted to enjoy a leisurely life in 'God's own country' with the money they had earned abroad. The majority of them, however, had neither human nor material resources to make a real contribution to Kerala's development. They not only had poor levels of general and technical education, but also lacked entrepreneurial abilities and leadership qualities. Most of them had spent a substantial portion of their savings and were seeking assistance to sustain their high standards of living.

An important factor in their favour was that they constituted a more disciplined and committed workforce than the general segment of 'conscientized' workers of Kerala. If it is possible to impart entrepreneurial and technical skills and leadership qualities to them and provide them the required capital, they could make a real contribution to Kerala's development. This is no doubt a tall order, the government at best could act as a facilitator in this effort.

Those who were more wealthy and were higher on human resources and entrepreneurial leadership qualities did not return to Kerala in considerable numbers. They have to be involved in the economic development of Kerala. In order to achieve this, however, an entirely new approach to NRKs is needed.

While the government expects assistance from return emigrants for the state's development, return emigrants, in turn, want the government's help for their own rehabilitation. In our view, they deserve help. When they were abroad they had made significant contribution to the state in terms of foreign remittances. Emigration has been the single most important factor in the otherwise dreary development scenario in Kerala in the last quarter of the last century. An emigrant who returned to Kerala in recent years had, on an average, earned around Rs. 7,50,000 during his sojourn abroad (6 years and 3 months). Their contribution to reducing unemployment and poverty levels and improving the housing conditions in the state has been widely acclaimed.

They have utilized a substantial portion of their savings for subsistence, buying land, constructing houses, paying dowries, repaying debts, etc. They invested their meagre resources in self-employment projects which yielded no income and a majority of these projects failed in course of time. Return emigrants remain a disillusioned group who hopes that the government would bail them out.

For nearly one-fifths of return emigrants, the emigration experience was a misadventure and as a result they lost their wealth, health and energy. There is no economic justification for any agency to provide social welfare assistance except to this small group. In general, the government may not find it justifiable to introduce social welfare programmes for return emigrants. Return emigrants have time and again proved that the financial assistance given to them by way of loans for small-scale industries did not cut much ice. Many of them want pension, but there is little justification for extending special treatment to them in preference to other deserving segments of the population.

On the basis of this study, two suggestions have been made for the rehabilitation of return emigrants, for those who have already come back and for those who would be returning in future. These are introducing a welfare scheme and organizing cooperatives for specific tasks (such as public works and tourism projects) which could profitably utilize the work discipline of return emigrants. The seed money for both these schemes should be provided by the commercial banks of Kerala which have received and continue to receive massive inflows of funds by way of emigrants' remittances. The maintenance of these schemes on a continuing basis should be the responsibility of emigrants (welfare schemes) and return emigrants (cooperatives) themselves. The role of the government in this should ideally be that of a facilitator.

References

Appleyard, Reginald T., 'Migration and Development: Myths and Reality,' *International Migration Review*, vol. 23, no. 3, 1989, pp. 486-99.

Azam, Farooq-i-Azam, *Re-integration of Return Migrants in Asia: A Review and Proposal*, New Delhi: ILO-ARTEP, 1987.

Commerce Research Bureau, *Emigration, Inward Remittances and Economic Growth of Kerala: Report of a Survey*, Bombay, 1978.

Ghosh, Bimal, ed., *Return Migration: Journey of Hope or Despair?*, IOM/UN, Geneva, 2000.

Government of Kerala, *Report on the Utilization of Gulf Remittances in Kerala*, Thiruvananthapuram: Department of Economics and Statistics, 1987.

———, *Report on Migration Survey, 1992-93*, Thiruvananthapuram: Department of Economics and Statistics, 1994.

Gunatilleke, Godfrey, ed., *Migration to the Arab World: Experience of Returning Migrants*, Tokyo: UNU Press, 1991.

Irudaya Rajan, S. and K.C. Zachariah, 'Long-term Implications of Low Fertility in Kerala', *Asia Pacific Population Journal*, vol. 13, no. 4, 1998, pp. 41-66.

Irudaya Rajan, S., 'From Kerala to the Gulf: Impacts of Labour Migration', *Asia Pacific Migration Journal*, vol. 13, no. 4, 2004, pp. 497-509.

Issac, T.M.T., 'Economic Consequences of the Gulf Crisis: A Study with Special Reference to Kerala', in *The Gulf Crisis and South Asia*, ed. P. Wickramasekera, New Delhi: UNDP/ARTEP, 1993.

King, Russel, ed., *Return Migration and Regional Economic Problems*, New Hampshire: Croom Helm, 1986.

Kurien, Raju, 'Patterns and Effects of Emigration from Kerala: A Study of Two Villages', M.Phil. dissertation, Centre for Development Studies, 1978.

Mathew, E.T. and P.R. Gopinathan Nair, 'Socio-economic Characteristics of Emigrants and Emigrants' Households: A Case Study of Two Villages in Kerala', *Economic and Political Weekly*, 15 July 1978, vol. 13, no. 28, pp. 1141-53.

Nair, P.R. Gopinathan, 'Asian Migration to the Middle East', in *Migration of Asian Workers to the Arab World*, ed. Godfrey Gunatilleke, Tokyo: UNU, 1986.

———, Chapter on 'India', in *Migration to the Arab World: Experience for Return Emigrants*, ed. Godfrey Gunatilleke, UNU: Tokyo, 1991.

———, 'Return of Overseas Contract Workers and Their Rehabilitation and Development in Kerala (India)', *International Migration*, Special Issue, January 1999, vol. 37, no. 1, pp. 209-40.

Nambiar, A.C.K., 'A Voyage to the Gulf and Back: Process and Its Outcome with Reference to Return Migrants', in *Indian Migration to the Middle East Trends, Patterns and Socio-economic Impacts*, ed. B.A. Prakash, Rohtak: Spellbound Publications, 1998.

Prakash, B.A., 'Impact of Foreign Remittances: A Case Study of Chavakkad Village', *Economic and Political Weekly*, 8 July 1978, vol. 16, no. 27, pp. 1107-11.

———, Gulf Emigration and Its Economic Impact: The Kerala Experience, *Economic and Political Weekly*, 12 December 1998, vol. 33, no. 50, pp. 3209-13.

Reyes, Belinda, *Dynamics of Immigration: Return Migration to Western Mexico*, San Fransisco: Public Policy Institute of California, 1997.

Saith, A., 'Absorbing External Shocks: The Gulf Crisis, International Migration Linkages and the Indian Economy 1990 (with Special Reference to the Impact on Kerala)', *Development and Change*, 1992, vol. 23, no. 1, pp. 101-46.

UNFPA, *Technical Symposium on International Migration and Development, 29 June – 3 July 1998*, New York: The Hague, 1998.

Zachariah, K.C., E.T. Mathew and S. Irudaya Rajan, 'Migration in Kerala State, India: Dimensions, Determinants and Consequences', Working Paper I, Thiruvanathapuram: Centre for Development Studies, 1999.

———, 'Migration in Kerala State, India: Dimensions, Determinants and Consequences', Working Paper II, Centre for Development Studies, Thiruvanathapuram, 2000.

———, 'Impact of Migration on Kerala's Economy and Society', *International Migration*, vol. 39, no. 1, 2001a, pp. 63-88.

———, 'Social, Economic and Demographic Consequences of Migration on Kerala', *International Migration*, vol. 39, no. 2, 2001b, pp. 43-72.

———, *Dynamics of Migration in Kerala, Dimensions, Determinants and Consequences*, Hyderabad: Orient Longman, 2003.

Zachariah, K.C. and S. Irudaya Rajan, 'Gulf Revisited', Centre for Development Studies (Thiruvananthapuram), Working Paper No. 363, 2001. www.cds.edu

———, 'Unemployment in Kerala at the Turn of the Century: Insights from CDS Gulf Migration Studies', Working Paper No. 374, Centre for Development Studies (Thiruvananthapuram). www.cds.edu

———, 'Gender Dimensions of Migration in Kerala: Macro and Micro Evidence', *Asia Pacific Population Journal*, 2001a, 16 (3), pp. 47-70.

———, 'Migration Mosaic in Kerala: Trends and Determinants', *Demography India*, 2001b, 30 (1), pp. 137-65.

Zachariah, K.C., B.A. Prakash and S. Irudaya Rajan, 'Gulf Migration Study: Employment Wages and Working Conditions of Kerala Emigrants in United Arab Emirates', Centre for Development Studies (Thiruvananthapuram) Working Paper No. 326, 2002. www.cds.edu

———, The Impact of Immigration Policy on Indian Contract Migrants: The Case of the United Arab Emirates, *International Migration*, vol. 41, no. 4, 2003, pp. 161-72.

———, 'Indian Workers in UAE: Employment, Wages and Working Conditions', *Economic and Political Weekly*, vol. XXXIX, no. 22, 29 May 2004, pp. 2227-34.

Zachariah, K.C., P.R. Gopinathan Nair and S. Irudaya Rajan, 'Return Emigrants in Kerala: Rehabilitation Problems and Development Potential', Centre for Development Studies (Thiruvananthapuram) Working Paper No. 319, 2001. www.cds.edu

Zachariah, K.C., K.P. Kannan and S. Irudaya Rajan, *Kerala's Gulf Connection: CDS Studies on International Labour Migration from Kerala State in India*, Centre for Development Studies (Thiruvananthapuram), Monograph Series, 2002.

APPENDIX I

Schedule Number

RETURN MIGRATION SURVEY 2001

SPONSORED BY
CENTRE FOR DEVELOPMENT STUDIES

1. RETURN MIGRANTS FROM EMIGRANTS ENUMERATED IN 1998 KMS
2. RETURN MIGRANTS ENUMERATED FROM THE RETURN MIGRANTS OF 1998 KMS
3. RETURN MIGRANTS FROM EMIGRANTS AFTER 1998 KMS
4. OTHER RETURN MIGRANTS
5. RETURN MIGRANTS OF 1998 KMS WHO COULD NOT BE SURVEYED

RETURN MIGRATION SURVEY

Schedule 1: Return Migrants

BLOCK A: IDENTIFICATION PARTICULARS

District .... Taluka ....

City/Panchayat .... Ward ....

Number .... House No. /House Name ....

Name of Informant ....

Details about visits to the household	1	2	3
Date(s) of Interview			
Time taken			
Name of Investigator			
Signature of the investigator			
Name of the supervisor			
Signature of the supervisor			

BLOCK B: PERSONAL DATE OF THE RETURNED EMIGRANT (REM)

201	Name	
202	Sex (Male – 1, Female – 2)	
203	Religion: (Hindu – 1, Muslim – 2, Syrian Christian – 3, Latin Christian – 4, Others – 5)	
204	Caste (Hindus) (SC/ST – 1, Nair – 2, Ezhava – 3, Brahmin – 4, Others – 5)	
205	Year of birth	
206	Age (in completed years)	
207	Year of first emigration	
208	Relationship of the REM to the head of the household (Head of the household – 1, Wife of head – 2, Unmarried Children – 3, Married Children – 4, Brother/Sister – 5, Others – 6)	
209	Marital status: (Never married – 1, Currently married – 2, Widowed – 3, Divorced / Separated – 4)	
210	Educational status (Below primary – 1, Primary – 2, Less than secondary – 3, Secondary – 4, Degree – 5)	

211 Education: Professional/technical/ vocational No technical training or Work experience – 1 Work experience without any formal training in* – 2 Certificate in* – 3 Diploma in* – 4 Degree in* – 5 *carpentry – (a), masonry – (b), electrician – (c), civil engineering – (d), mechanical engineering – (e), architect – (f), medicine – (g), laboratory technician – (h), accountancy – (i), book keeping – (j), computer – (k) any other (specify)	

WORK EXPERIENCE: JUST BEFORE EMIGRATION

212	Economic activity status before emigration (Regular employment – 1, Casual employment – 2, self employed – 3, Unemployed seeking work – 4, Unemployed available for work – 5, Others – 6)	
213	Current Occupation (Describe)	
214	Period of service (years and months) If code 1, 2 or 3 against item 212 Economic sector in which worked: (Agriculture, Animal Husbandary, Fisheries etc. – 1, Mining and quarrying – 2, Manufacturing – 3, Trade commerce, hotels and Restaurants – 4, Transport – 5, Construction – 6, Service – 7, Others – 8)	
216	Annual Salary or wages or income: (Rs.)	
217	How many times you have gone outside India?	

218 Which are the countries?

	Country	No. of years
1st Trip		
2nd Trip		
3rd Trip		
4th Trip		
5th Trip		

DETAILS OF EMPLOYMENT ABROAD
(LAST JOB ONLY)

219 Country where employed

220 Occupation (Describe)

221 Period of service: (Years and months)

222 Economic sector in which the last job was pursued:
[Agriculture and other primary sector – 1, Mining and quarrying – 2, Manufacturing – 3, Trade, Commerce, Hotels and restaurants – 4, transport – 5, Construction – 6, Service – 7, Others – 8]

223 Annual salary or wages or income (Rs)

BLOCK C: PRE EMIGRATION PHASE

301 Reasons for seeking employment abroad (Write the first three reasons according to priority)

First ☐ Second ☐ Third ☐

Reasons
[Lack of employment opportunities in Kerala – 1, To improve living standards (such as higher level of consumption, better housing, own a car, and modern consumer durable) – 2, To redeem personal/family debts – 3, To discharge family responsibilities (e.g. marriage, higher education of daughters, sisters, brothers, etc.) – 4, To accumulate funds for investment in business – 5, To experience pleasures of travel and life in foreign countries – 6, others (specify) – 7]

302 Sources of Information about Employment Opportunities abroad
(Circle yes or no against relevant item)

Media: Newspapers/ TV/ Radio	Yes	No
Friends/relatives employed abroad	Yes	No
Recruiting Agencies	Yes	No
Emigrants on home leave or Emigrants who had returned	Yes	No
Others (specify)	Yes	No

303 Means by which first employment was secured (write the code in the box space) (direct application – 1, through Government Agencies – 2, through licensed recruiting agencies – 3, through unlicensed recruiting agencies – 4, through construction firms – 5, through friends and relatives – 6, through other contacts – 7, by means of visiting visa – 8, through pilgrimage – 9, other means – 10) ☐

304 Type of contract of employment entered into with the code in this box space ☐

[formal contract specifying terms and conditions of work and living – 1, letter or other communications from employer mentioning major terms of employment – 2, no formal contract/ only informal arrangements – 3, others (specify) – 4]

305 Language of contract:
[English – 1, Arabic – 2, Others – 3]

306 Whether advice/counselling received regarding terms and conditions before signing the contract
[Yes – 1, No – 2]

307 If Yes, from which source (Circle the appropriate entries)

1	friends	Yes	No
2	relatives	Yes	No
3	previous employer	Yes	No
4	voluntary agencies	Yes	No
5	governmental agencies	Yes	No
6	others(specify)	Yes	No

308 Was the advice/counselling helpful? Yes – 1 No – 2

BLOCK D: COSTS AND FINANCING OF MIGRATON

401 In connection with your emigration what were your costs. Give the costs under the following items. Write 'Nil' if no payment is made under any item

401a. Payment to recruitment agencies	Rs.	
401b. Payment to other intermediaries	Rs.	
401c. Passport	Rs.	
401d. Visa	Rs.	

401e. Air Ticket	Rs.	
401f. Emigration Clearance	Rs.	
401g. Loss due to fraud or cheating	Rs.	

402 Total cost of your last emigration Rs. [ ]

403 Sources of financing (circle the relevant items)

403a. Personal Savings	Yes	No
403b. Parents Savings	Yes	No
403c. Borrowing from friends/relatives	Yes	No
403d. Loans from moneylenders	Yes	No
403e. Loans from Banks	Yes	No
403f. Sale/mortgage of landed property	Yes	No
403g. Sale/pledging of financial assets	Yes	No
403h. Sale/pledging of ornaments or jewellery	Yes	No
403i. Government assistance	Yes	No
403j. Others (specify)	Yes	No

BLOCK E: EMPLOYMENT, WORK AND LIVING CONDITION ABROAD

501 Did you have any problems on arrival with the following (Circle the relevant items)

501a. Passport	Yes	No
501b. Visa	Yes	No
501c. Work permit	Yes	No

502 Whom did you make contact with on arrival? (Circle the relevant items)

1. Employer/employer's representatives	Yes	No
2. Friends/relatives	Yes	No
3. Indian embassy	Yes	No

503 Was the employment you received the same as the one promised at the time of recruitment?
[Yes – 1, No – 2]

504 In comparison with contracts offered to persons from other countries were the terms and conditions of your contract
[More Favourable – 1, The Same – 2, Less Favourable – 3]

505 Did you have to sign a second contract after arrival abroad?
[Yes – 1, No –2]

506 Were you allowed to keep your passport and other documents with you or were they taken away by the employer
[Allowed to keep with me – 1, Not allowed to keep with me – 2]

507 How was your housing accommodation
[Good quality – 1, Adequate – 2, Poor – 3]

508 Did you share your housing accommodation with others?
[With none, had independent accommodation – 1, Shared with others – 2]

509 How was the quality your food?
[Excellent – 1, Good – 2, Poor – 3]

510 Was your food free , subsidised, or of market value?
[Free – 1, Subsidised – 2, Market value – 3]

511 How was the medical care you received?
[Good – 1, Satisfactory – 2, Poor – 3, No medical help – 4]

512 How was educational facilities in your place of work?
[Good – 1, Satisfactory – 2, Poor – 3, No facilities – 4]

513 Were there facilities/ freedom for religious observances?
[Yes – 1, No – 2]

514 Did your spouse live with you in the host country/countries?
[Yes – 1, No – 2]

515 If yes it item 514, Was she employed?
[Yes – 1, No – 2]

516 If no in item 514, What were the reasons for not taking the wife? Choose the appropriate one from the following
[Lack of accommodation – 1, Insufficient income – 2, Desire to maximise savings – 3, Difficulty in getting job for the spouse – 4, Spouse employed at home – 5, Restrictions by host country – 6, Permission denied by India – 7, Education of children – 8, Unwillingness of spouse – 9]

517 Did you ever sought assistance from Indian consulate in the host country for any matters?
[Yes – 1, No – 2]

518 If 'Yes' in item 517 what sort of assistance?
Circle the appropriate ones

About grievances and dispute with employer	
Problems of remittances	
Problems of communication with people at home	
Legal problems in the host country	
Others (specify)	

519 Were you satisfied with the assistance got from the consulate?
[Yes – 1, No – 2]

520 Your average income per month

520a. Salary or from Business	Rs.	
520b. Income from other sources	Rs.	
520c. Total income	Rs.	

521 Your average living expense per month

522 Your average monthly remittances to home

523 Who was mainly responsible in managing your household when you were away?
[Spouse – 1, Parents of emigrants – 2, Parents of Spouse – 3, other relative (specify) – 4]

524 Did you send any remittance home when you were working abroad?
[Yes – 1, No – 2]

525 If YES, To whom did you send the money?
[Circle all the appropriate codes]

Spouse	1
Your parents	2
Spouse's parents	3
Others	4

526 What was the channel through which the money was sent? [Circle all the appropriate codes]

Through friends	1
Through banks	2
Mail transfer	3
NRI deposits	4

527 Did the you have any experience of getting cheated by in the transfer of remittances?
[Yes – 1, No – 2]

528 If yes, in item 524, which agency ? [Friends/relatives/neighbour – 1, Financial institutions other than commercial banks – 2, Commercial banks – 3]

529 Do you have any of the following bank accounts now?
[Yes – 1, No – 2] [Circle all the appropriate codes]

529a. Current Account	1	2
529b. Savings Account	1	2
529c. Fixed Account	1	2

530 Did you have any of the following bank accounts before emigration?
[Yes – 1, No – 2] [Circle all the appropriate codes]

530a. Current Account	1	2
530b. Savings Account	1	2
530c. Fixed Account	1	2

531 What were the problems faced by your household back home during your stay abroad?
[Yes – 1, No – 2] [Circle all the appropriate codes]

531a. Illness in the family	1	2
531b. Death	1	2
531c. Loss of Assets	1	2
531d. Threats to personal safety	1	2
531e. Disputes	1	2

BLOCK F : POST RETURN MIGRATION PHASE

601 Year of your return from abroad. [ ]

602 What was the reasons for your final return?
[Yes – 1, No – 2] [Circle all the appropriate codes]

602a. Expiry of contract	1	2
602b. Resigned job due to difficult living conditions abroad	1	2
602c. Resigned job due to difficult working conditions abroad	1	2
602d. Job terminated by employer before termination of contract	1	2
602e. Political upheaval	1	2
602f. Illegal stay abroad and compulsory repatriation	1	2
602g. Conditions at home required the REM's presence	1	2
602h. Ill-health	1	2
602i. Injury/accident/ Incapacitation	1	2

603. Did you receive any special skills while working abroad?
[Yes – 1, No – 2] [ ]

604 If 'yes', in item 603 what was the type of skills?
[Circle all the appropriate codes]

Craft skills	1
Technical skills	2
Supervisory/managerial skills	3
Professional	4

House keeping	5
Public relations	6
Others	7

605. Has the experience/skills acquired abroad been of use to you on your return?
[Yes – 1, No – 2]

606. What form you keep your savings?
[Yes – 1, No – 2] [Circle all the appropriate codes]

In banks	1	2
In other financial assets	1	2
mutual funds, shares, savings, certificates	1	2
In other non-banking financial institutions	1	2
with private financiers, blade companies etc.	1	2

607 Have you invested money on any of the following items? Write the amount spent. Write 'Nil' in case no amount was spent

607a. Purchase of agricultural land	Rs.	
607b. Construction of buildings	Rs.	
607c. Marriage of sisters/ Brothers/daughters	Rs.	
607d. Higher education of children	Rs.	

608 What is your activity status now? That is, Are you now:
[Self Employed/Employee – 1, Unemployed seeking employment – 2, Unemployed not seeking but available for employment – 3, Not in labour force (students, housewife, pensioner etc.) – 4]

609 If gainfully employed, i.e. code 1 in item 608, Do you have
[Regular employment – 1, Casual employment – 2, Self employment – 3]

610 In what economic sector are you employed now?
[Agriculture, Animal Husbandary, Fisheries etc. – 1, Mining and quarrying – 2, Manufacturing – 3, Trade commerce, hotels and Restaurants – 4, Transport – 5, Construction – 6, Service – 7, Others – 8]

611 What is your occupation? (describe)

IF SELF EMPLOYED

612 How much money have you invested in your business?

613 Was the money entirely your own or others also?
[Own – 1, Partly from others – 2, wholly from others – 3]

614 Did you seek any assistance from public institutions?
[Yes – 1, No – 2]

615 If 'yes' to item 614 from what source did you seek assistance?
[Government – 1, Banks – 2, NGOs – 3, Others – 4, More than one source – 5]

616 What type of assistance you sought from these institutions ?

Type of assistance	616 Circle appropriate ones	617 If circle in 616, Did you get assistance? [Yes – 1, No – 2]	618 If 'Yes' in item 617, from which agency? [Code]
Financial	1		
Technical	2		
Marketing	3		
Raw material	4		
Identification of business	5		
Job placement	6		
Training	7		

[Agency code: Banks – 1, State agencies (specify) – 2, Voluntary agencies (specify) – 3, Friends – 4, Businessman – 5, Others (Specify) – 6]

619 Were you engaged in any economic activity other than the present one between the time you returned and the present employment?
[Yes – 1, No – 2]

620 If yes to item 619 during which years?

621 If yes to item 619 what type of employment did you have?
[Self employment – 1, Regular employment – 2, Casual Employment – 3]

622 Why did you give that employment?
[not profitable enough – 1, had labour problems – 2, better opportunities came – 3, other reasons (specify) – 4]

IF UNEMPLOYED

623 After you return from abroad, were you at any time engaged in gainful employment?
[Yes – 1, No – 2]

624 Why did you discontinue that activity?
[Not remunerative enough – 1, had labour problems – 2, financial problems – 3, Other reasons(specify) – 4]

625 After your return did you ever try to start a shop, or industry or some other business of your own in which you could be self employed?
[Yes – 1, No – 2]

626 If yes to item 625 why it did not succeed?
[Not enough money – 1, Scarcity of workers – 2, Labour militancy – 3, High wage rate – 4, Marketing Problem – 5, Power shortage – 6, Lack of transportation facilities – 7, politicians' interference – 8, Lack of credit facilities – 9, Lack of Raw materials – 10, Other (Specify) – 11]

627 Did you ever approach Government agencies for help in starting a business of your own?
[Yes – 1, No – 2]

628 If Yes, to item 627 what was the result?
[Got help – 1, Did not get any help – 2]

IF THE PERSONS IS UNEMPLOYED AND DID NOT SEEK EMPLOYMENT OR WAS AVAILABLE FOR EMPLOYMENT

629 Why you did not seek employment?
[Too old to work – 1, Wanted to study – 2, Enough money, and there was no need

to get money by working – 3, Can't cope with the working conditions in Kerala – 4, Labour militancy in Kerala – 5, Political interference – 6, High wage rates – 7, Want to follow an easy life – 8, Other reasons (Specify) – 9]

ASK ALL RETURN MIGRANTS

630 Some people think that the Government should do more than what they are doing now to rehabilitate and resettle the Return Emigrants. What is your view in this matter?
[Yes, Government should do more – 1, No, there is no need – 2, No comments – 3]

631 What do you expect from the Government to rehabilitate the Return migrants? [Describe]

BLOCK G: PERCEPTIONS OF JOBS IN THE FOREIGN COUNTRIES

701	What is the opinion about Employment prospects in Gulf countries? [Declining – 1, Remain unchanged – 2, increasing – 3]	
702	In your opinion what type of skills are most in demand now? [Unskilled labour – 1, Skilled – 2]	
703	Is the average salary/wages for the migrants? [Falling – 1, Remain unchanged – 2, Rising – 3]	
704	Is the living expenses of the migrants in Gulf countries? [Declining – 1, Remain unchanged – 2, increasing – 3]	
705	Is Competition from other migrant - sending countries? [Declining – 1, Remain unchanged – 2, increasing – 3]	
706	What is your overall assignment of emigration experience? [Was very good – 1, Was not good – 2, Was harmful – 3]	
707	If you get an offer now to emigrate, would you accept the offer? [Yes – 1, No – 2]	
708	If your son or brother ask your advice about migrating to one of the Gulf countries, will you? [Encourage – 1, Discourage – 2]	

APPENDIX II

Schedule Number

KERALA MIGRATION SURVEY 1998
KERALA STATE—INDIA

CENTRE FOR DEVELOPMENT STUDIES

Migration Status: Write the answers as 0, 1, 2, etc. from Block 5 and 6

1. RETURN MIGRANTS FROM OUTSIDE INDIA
2. EMIGRANTS LIVING OUTSIDE INDIA
3. RETURN MIGRANTS OTHER STATES OF INDIA
4. OUT-MIGRANTS FROM OTHER STATES IN INDIA

MIGRATION SURVEY

Consequences of International Migration

Schedule 1

BLOCK 1

Identification Particulars

District .... Taluka ....

City/Panchayat .... Ward ....

Number .... House No. /House Name ....

Name of Informant ....

Details about visits to the household	1	2
Date of Interview		
Name of Investigator		
Name of the supervisor		
Time taken		

The respondent should be the head of the household.
If the head of the household is not present, the information should be collected from the immediate responsible person.

BLOCK 2

File name:
Details about households

01	02	03	04	05	06	07	08	09	10
Serial No		*Relationship with the Head*	*Sex*	*Date of Birth*	*Place of Birth*	*Educational Status*	*15 year or above*		*Classification*
							Occupational Status	*Marital Status*	
1.									
2.									
3.									
4.									
5.									
6.									
7.									
8.									
9.									
10.									

Codes:

Column 03

1. Head of the Household
2. Husband/Wife
3. Unmarried children
4. Married children
3. Son in law/Daughter in law
6. Grand child
7. Father/Mother/Mother in law

Column 04

1. Male
2. Female

Column 06

1. In Kerala
2. Outside Kerala within India
3. Outside India

Column 07

1. Illiterate
2. Literate without school Education
3. Primary
4. UP to lower secondary
5. Secondary passed but no other qualification
6. Degree holders
7. Primary incomplete

Column 08

1. Employed in State /Central Govt.
2. Employed in Semi Govt. Aided school/college, co-operative /local administrative bodies.
3. Employed in Private sector
4. Self employment
5. Unpaid family work
6. Agricultural labour
7. Coolies in non-agri. Sector
8. Job seekers
9. Job not required
10. Student
11. HHold duties →
12. Old age/Pensioners

Column 09

1. Unmarried
2. Married
3. Widow/Widower
4. Divorced
5. Separated

Column 10

1. Married women with age less than 40
2. Male/Female above 60
3. Married women with husbands outside Kerala

BLOCK 3
MIGRATION STATUS

01	11	12	13	14	15	16	17
Serial No.	*Ever lived outside Kerala for a period of one year or more?*	*Ever lived outside Kerala for less than a year for work/looking for work/for studies*	*If there is anybody in Column 11 and/or Column 12*				*If "Yes" to Ques No. 16 from where did he get financial support to come back*
			Where was the person living before coming to Kerala	*Residence code*	*When did the person come back to India*	*Whether the person came back to India on the basis of declaration of amnesty*	
1.							
2.							
3.							
4.							
5.							
6.							
7.							
8.							

Codes:

Column 11

1. Yes 2. No

Column 12

1. Yes 2. No

Column 13

1. Abu Dhabi—UAE
2. Dubai—UAE
3. Saudi Arabia—Jeddah
4. Kuwait & Alian
5. Muscat
6. Oman
7. Qatar
8. Bahrain
9. Sharjah—UAE
10. Iraq & Iran
11. South East Asia—Philippines, Malaysia, Singapore, Hongkong
12. Latin America, Carebian Islands & West Indies
13. Nepal, Bangladesh, Srilanka, Maldives & Pakistan
14. USA
15. Europe
16. Africa
17. Australia
18. Others

States in India

19. Andhra Pradesh
20. Assam
21. Bihar
22. Gujarat
23. Karnataka
24. Madhya Pradesh
25. Maharashtra
26. Orissa
27. Punjab
28. Rajasthan
29. Tamil Nadu
30. Uttar Pradesh
31. West Bengal
32. Delhi
33. Pondicherry
34. Others

Column 14

1. Within India
2. Outside India

Column 16

1. Yes 2. No

Column 17

1. No support (Self)
2. Government
3. Others

BLOCK 4
EMIGRATION AFTER 1980

01	18	19	20	21	22	23	24	25		26	27	28
Serial No.	*Resident of this house who have gone out of Kerala after 1980 and stays there still?*	*Relationship of the member wtih the head of the HHold*	*Sex*	*Name of the State/ Country presently residing*	*Reason for going to other states/ abroad*	*When did you go outside Kerala for the first time?*	*Age when you first went outside Kerala*	*Ecuational status at time of emigration/ out migration*		*Marital status at the time of emi-gration/ out migra-tion*	*Occupation at status at the time of emi-gration/ out migra-tion*	*Occupation-al Status at present*
								A	B			

Codes: For columns 19, 20, 21, 26, 27 and 28 use the same codes used in Block 2 and Block 3

Column 22

1. For job
2. For seeking job
3. To stay with relatives
4. For studies
5. Other reasons

BLOCK 5
RETURNED MIGRANTS

29.1. Returned from Abroad

	1	2	3	4
Serial No. As in block 2				
Name As in block 2				

29.2. Returned from other states

	1	2	3	4
Name As in block 2				

BLOCK 6
CURRENT MIGRANTS

30.1. Persons residing Abroad

	1	2	3	4
Serial No. As in block 4; Columns 18 and 21				
Name As in block 2 As in block 4; Columns 18 and 21				

30.2. Persons residing in other states

	1	2	3	4
Name As in block 2 As in block 4; Columns 18 and 21				

BLOCK 7
EXPENSE FOR MIGRATION (FOR THOSE WHO HAD GONE ABROAD)

Qn. 31

	1	2	*3*	*4*
Name				
Travelling expenses				
Visa cost				
Commission to agents				
Loss due to cheating				
Total				

BLOCK 8
SOURCES FOR SPENDING FOR MIGRATION ABROAD

Qn. 32

	1	2	*3*	*4*
Item				
From own savings				
From family members				
Borrowing from friends/relatives/bank				
By selling gold ornaments etc.				
By selling landed property				
Others				

BLOCK 9
QUESTIONS TO HOUSEHOLD MEMBERS

33. During the last one year did you or any member of your family receive money or goods from any persons who is living outside India?
    1. Yes Go to question 34
    2. No Go to question 37

34. How much money you have received from emigrants during the last 12 months?
    Total from all emigrants ....

35.1. Kind of goods you received
    (If there are more than one answer enter it in 35.2)
    1. Clothing
    2. Gold ornaments
    3. Light electricals
    4. VCR, TV and similar heavy electricals
    5. Others

35.2. Kind of goods you received
    1. Clothing
    2. Gold ornaments
    3. Light electricals
    4. VCR, TV and similar heavy electricals
    5. Others

35.3 Total value of goods .... (Estimate)

36.1 How was this money used?
    1. To meet living expenses of the family
    2. To meet educational purposes
    3. To pay back debt incurred to buy ticket, Visa, etc.
    4. To buy land
    5. To pay dowry of relatives
    6. To build or renovate house
    7. To start a business
    8. Agricultural purposes
    9. Deposited in Banks
    10. Others (Specify) ____________

BLOCK 10
HOUSEHOLD ARTICLES

37. Is your house electrified?
    1. Yes   2. No
38. What type of fuel is used for cooking?
    1. Wood
    2. Electricity
    3. Kerosine
    4. Others
    5. L.P.G
39. What type of toilet facilities do you have in the house?
    1. Flush
    2. Pit
    3. Common latrine facility
    4. No latrine facility
40. Does any member of this HH owns a house here or elsewhere?
    1. Yes   2. No
41. When was this house constructed or bought?
    Year ......
42. Did you take any loan from Govt. or Bank or any other institution to construct or buy your house?
    1. Yes   2. No
43. Did you get any money from abroad for constructing your house?
    1. Yes   2. No
44. What is the approximate cost of construction of this house?
    1. Below Rs. 20,000
    2. Between 20,000 and 1,00,000
    3. Between 1,00,000 and 5,00,000
    4. Above 5,00,000
45. Type of house which the HH is now occupying
    1. Luxurious
    2. Very Good (2 bed rooms with attached bathrooms, concrete roof, Mosaic floor)
    3. Good (1 bed room, brick and cement walls, concrete or tile roof)
    4. Poor (Brick walls, cement floor, tin or asbestos roof)
    5. Kutcha (Mud walls, Mud floor & Thatched roof)
46. How much land, Agricultural & Non-Agricultural together is owned by the members of this HH
    1. Wet land (cents) ....
    2. Dry land (cents) ....
    3. Total (Cents) ....

47. Does the family own any of the following

1. Motor car	Yes	No
2. Taxi	Yes	No
3. Truck	Yes	No
4. Motor Cycle /Scooter	Yes	No
5. Telephone	Yes	No
6. Television	Yes	No
7. VCR/VCP	Yes	No
8. Radio/Transistor	Yes	No
9. Sofa set	Yes	No
10. Water pump	Yes	No
11. Sewing Machine	Yes	No
12. Fridge	Yes	No
13. Washing Machine	Yes	No
14. Fan	Yes	No
15. Mixie/Grinder	Yes	No
16. Toaster	Yes	No
17. Gas stove/Electric range	Yes	No
18. Clock	Yes	No
19. Electric Iron	Yes	No
20. Camera	Yes	No
21. Stereo system	Yes	No
22. Watch	Yes	No
23. Cycle	Yes	No

48. What is your religion & caste.
    1. Scheduled caste/tribe
    2. Nair
    3. Ezhawa
    4. Syrian Christian
    5. Latin Christian
    6. Shia Muslim
    7. Sunni Muslim
    8. Others
    9. Nadar Hindu

APPENDIX III

LIST OF RETURN EMIGRANT MALAYALEE ASSOCIATIONS IN KERALA

NON RESIDENT INDIAN WELFARE ASSOCIATION (NRIWA),
V.C. Ram Mohan
(Director-Operations)
P.B. No. 6, Ambalapuzha,
Alappuzha-688561

GULF MALAYALI RETURNED ASSOCIATION
Trissur District Committee
c/o Mr. Sreekumar S.
(Convenor)
Lakshmi Nivas, Koodappuzha
Chalakkudy-680307

GULF MALAYALI RETURNED ASSOCIATION
Ernakulam District Committee
c/o Mr. T. K. Ashokan
(President)
Thykottathil, Ayyampilly P.O.
Kochi-682501

GULF MALAYALI RETURNED ASSOCIATION
Krishnapuram Panchayat Unit
Kappil East, Krishnapuram
Kayamkulam

INDIAN OVERSEAS CONGRESS
Mukundapuram Taluk Committee
Jose Puthenpurakkal
(President)
IOC, Chalkkudy, Pottah P.O.
Thrissur-680722

PRAVASI SANGHOM
(Idukki District) Committee
Gemini Tourist Complex
P.B. No. 22
Thodupuzha-685584

KOTTAYAM JILLA PRAVASI SANGHOM
Regent Plaza,
B/16, CMS College Road
Kottayam-1

KERALA PRAVASI SANGHAMAM
State Committee
15/14 Karuvelippadi
Kochi-68205

KERALA PRAVASI SANGHAMAM
Ernakulam District Committee,
Vattathussery House,
Murikkumpadam, Azheekkal P.O.
Kochi-682510

GULF RETURNEES WELFARE CO-OPERATIVE SOCIETY LTD.
No. S. 307, Hosdurg
Kanhangad - 671315
Kasaragod

GULF RETURNEES WELFARE ASSOCIATION
S.A. Aboo Backer
(President)
Kornish Castle, Opp. K.R.S,
R.C. Road-32
Kasaragod

ALL KERALA GULF RETURNEES COORDINATION COMMITTEE
c/o P.P. Ahmed Kutty
(Convenor)
Alinchuvadu, Jas Manzil
P.O. Velimukku

Sri N.J. Satheesh Chandra Babu
(President)
All India Gulf Returnees Association
Kaithakode Unit
Santhi Bhavan, Kaithacodu P.O.
Kollam-691543

Sri Gopalakrishnan S.
(President)
Non Resident Indians and Returnees Association
Aswathy
Poovattoor West, Mavady P.O.
691507

Kuwait and Gulf Returnees Organisation
Beena Shopping Complex
Vembayam P.O.
Thiruvananthapuram-695615

Gulf returnees and NRIs Association
Ampanad Buildings
Thengamam P.O.
Adoor (Via), Pathanamthitta District

Sri Shoukath
Kaniamparambil
Opposite Juma Masjid
Vellakinen
Alappuzha

Sri Vellayani Sreekumar
(President)
Pravasi Malayalee Welfare Association
T.C. 14/1364, Paris Road, Bakery Junction
Vikas Bhavan P.O.
Thiruvananthapuram-33

EX-GULF WELFARE ASSOCIATION (EGWA)
District Committee, Malappuram
Hassan Sageer
(President)
c/o IUML Office, P.O. Down Hill, Malappuram

KERALA STATE PRAVASI LEAGUE
E.K. Jalaludeen
(Convenor)
E.K. house, Bara Valappu
Main Road, Thalassery

GULF RETURNEES AND EMPLOYEES ORGANISATION
Emirate Press, Kallai Road
Kozhikode.

KUWAIT NON-RESIDENT KERALITES UN COMPENSATION BENEFICIARIES FORUM
9/904 Half Velluvambaram
Malappuram-673651

VIPRAVASI PRATHIKARANA VEDI (VPPV)
Paravanadukkam Post
Kasaragod-671317

INDIAN OVERSEAS RETURNEES CONGRESS
Prof. Mathew Korah
(President)
25/171, Union Club Road
Kottayam

THE PAYYANNUR GULF MENS WELFARE CO-OP. SOCIETY
No. C 1115, P.O. Payyannur,
Kannur-670307

Sri Ajithkumar Menon
2/35 Surabhi
V. N. Puram, Ambikapuram Post
Palakkad-11

EX-GULF WELFARE ASSOCIATION, MULLASSERY
P.O. Mullassery,
Chavakkad, Thrissur-680509

GULF RETURNEES WELFARE ASSOCIATION
Kannur, K.P. Janardhanan Nambiar
(Secy) Aaroodam,
Chovva, P.O. Kannur-6

GULF RETURNED AND GULF WORKING MALAYALEE'S ASSOCIATION-KERALA.
P. Raveendran
(President)
Pandhayil House, panampad
Porengu, P.O. Malappuram-679584

GULF RETURNEE ASSOCIATION OF TRAVANCORE,
Flat No. 9, E. John Philopose Nagar,
Housing Board Colony
IInd Stage, Tiruvalla

VIDESH
P. Janarchanan
(President)
Mattathil House, Muthalakkodan
P.O. Thodupuzha,
Idukki-685605

ALL KERALA FOREIGN RETURNEES CENTRE
165, Hill Gardens
P.O. Kuttanellore
Thrissur

Sri S. Ahmed
(President)
All Kerala Gulf Returnees Organisation State Committee
Bismi, T.C 35/1058
Gandhi Nagar, Vallakadav
Trivandrum-695008

Sri P.M. Sethumadhava Menon
(President)
Kerala Pravasi Returnees Congress Council
Malappuram District Committee
Kanhiramukku P.O.
Malapputam District, Pin. 679584

Sri George Parakkal
(President)
All India Gulf Returnees &

Sri Indianoor Hamsa
(President)
Federation of Foreign Returnees

Employees Association
27/1282, Mount Tabore Building
Vanchiyoor
Trivandrum

Sri George Abraham
(General Secretary)
Foreign Employed and Returned Malayalis
(FERMA)
XXX/936, Appose Complex
Near YMCA
Pathanamthitta-689645

Sri Chacka Ravi
(General Secretary)
All Kerala Pravasi Malayalee Welfare Association
TC 36/1074
West Fort
Trivandrum

Sri Kattaikonam Rajan
(Secretary)
All Kerala Gulf Returnees Federation
TC 41/2336(16)
MRC Complex, Opposite Span Hospital
Manacad P.O.

Sri K. Sasidharan
(President)
Kerala Gulf Returnees' Association
Chirayinkeezh, Chirayinkeezh P.O.
Thiruvananthapuram District
Pin 695304

Sri Najeeb
(Secretary)
Malappuram Sangam Pravasi Sangam
Uphill, Malappuram

Organisation
Lakshmi Nagar
E-2 Pattom Palace P.O.
Thiruvananthapuram-695004

Vidheesa Malayalee Cultural Forum
c/o Sri Mankulam Jayaprakash
(President)
Mangalapallil
Elampal P.O.
Punalur

Sri M.P. Moideen
(General Secretary)
Kerala State Ex Gulf Welfare Association
Kozhikode District Committee
League Centre
Kurial Lane, Kozhikode-673032

Sri Sajith Kumar
(Secretary)
Mother Theresa Memorial Charitable Society
c/o Kollamvilakom
Chirayinkeezhu P.O.
Trivandrum District

Smt. V.P. Zuhra
(President)
Pravasi Malayali Vanitha Council
34/652A, Civil Station P.O.
Kozhikode-673020

Sri C.A. Muhammed Rafi
(President)
Non Resident Indians & Returnees' Association
Mabrooq, Edamon P.O.
Punalor
Kollam District

Sri P. Muhammad Shafi
(President)
Gulf Returnees Welfare Association
State Committee
Thikkadappuram, Neeleswaram
Kasaragod District

Sri P.R. Kishore
(President)
Pravasi Accademy & Community Development Society
Anakkayam, Anakkayam, P.O.
Munduparambu (Via)
Malappuram District
Pin 676509

Sri Abdhul Razak
(President)
Kerala Muslim Cultural Centre
Wayanad District Co-ordination Committee
Kalpetta, P.O. 673121

President
Wayanad District Pravasi Sangom
Near woodlands
Main Road Kalpetta P.O.
Wayanad-673121

Sri P.M.A. Azeez
(President)
Kasargod Jilla Gulf Returnees & Welfare Association
Shukkoor Building
Kottachery P.O. Kanhangad
Kasaragod-671315

Sri V.G. Balakrishnan
(President)
All Kerala Pravasi Malayalee Association
Sri Sailam Shopping complex
Azhoor Road
Pathanamthitta-689645

Sri T.P. Antony
(President)
Kerala Pravasi Sangamam
State Committee
15/14 Karuvelippadi
Cochin-682005

Sri Issac Thomas
(President)
Gulf Returnees Association of Travancore
Flat No. 9 E. John Philipose Nagar
IInd Stage, R.S.P.O.
Thiruvalla
Ph. 630407

Dheseeya Gulf Returnees Organisation
'Nandavanam'
Thiruvallom P.O.
Thiruvananthapuram-695027

Sri Y.S.G. James
(President)
Kairali Pravasi Association
Registered Office
ARA81, Devasam Board Junction
Kavadiyar P.O. Trivandrum-3

Sri Samad Mankada
(President)
Pravasi Malayalee & Gulf Returnees Association
Mankada Area Committee
Mankada P.O.
Malappuram District
Kerala

Sri U.K. Khadeer Ravuthar
(Chairman)
Gulf Returnees Rehabilitation Trust, Mullamangalam
Madathara
Kollam-691541

Sri Indianoor Hamsa
(President)
Gulf Returnees Organisation
(GRO)
Regd Office
c/o Indianoor Hamsa
Indianoor, Kottakkal-676503

Sri K.G. Sathyaseelan
(President)
Pravasi Council
Pravasi Bhavan
Darussalam Complex, Thriprayar
Nattika P.O., Thrissur 680566

Sri Dwimani
(President)
All Kerala Gulf Returnees
Association (AKGRA)
Baby Madom
Vakkom P.O.
Pin 695308

Sri S. Girija Sankar
(President)
Gulf Returnees Welfare
Association
Registered Office
BNRA 30, Balavan Nagar
Manacaud, Trivandrum

Sri Achuthan Mavelikkara
(Gen. Secretary)
Gulf Malayalee Returned
Association
Panutharayil
Ponnezha, Thekkekara P.O.
Mavelikkara-7
2328380

Sri Jacob T.K. Vaidyan
(President)
Non-Resident Indians and
Returnees Organisation Gulf
Returnees Welfare Association
Thengumvilayil
Thevalakkara P.O.
Kollam-690524

Pravasi Malayalee Council
Shyamala Complex
1st Floor, Near Training School
Kannur

Sri P.K. Kunheethutty
(President)
Gulf Keralites' Welfare Association
Alinchuvadu, Payyangadi
Tirur-676108

Sri K.L. Pillai
(President)
Gulf Keralites' Welfare Association
Regd. Office
Karthika Building,
Pallarimangalam P.O.
Mavelikkara-690107

Sri A.A. Salam
(State President)
All India Gulf Returnees
Association
Sharmila's
Lekshminada
Kollam-691014

Sri Attakoya Pallikandi
(Chairman)
Indo Arab Confederation Council
Regd. Office
Emirate Building, Kallai Road
Calicut-2

Sri Priyads
(Official spokesperson)
World Malayalee Council
Chennilode
Mecical College Post
Trivandrum

Sharjah Indian Association
c/o Sri Samuel P. George
(President)
Gil-Gal Plamootil
Pulimukku
Avaneeswaram
Kollam-17

Adv. R.V. Said Muhamad
(President)
Ex. Gulf Malayalee Association
Sree Ram Building
Poonkunnam
Thrissur-2

Sri Prasad Punnus
(President)
Pravasi Malayalee Council
Pravasi Bhavan
Thangal's Complex, C.H. Cross Road
Nadakkavu, Kozhikode-673001

PRAVASI ORGANISATION
V. Thambi
(President)
'Sharon'
Ainoor, Pazhanji
Thrissur-695004

PRAVASI MALAYAEE CONSORTIUM
8-A-2, Samarias Centre
PMG Jn. Pattom Palace P.O.
Thiruvananthapuram-695004

THRISSUR DISTRICT PRAVASI SANGHAM
Sri R.V. Abdhul Rahim
(President)
Puthen purayil House, Karakkad,
Guruvayoor Thrissur

Sri Abdhul Jabbar
(President)
Association of Kerala Unemployed
Gulf Returnees Rehabilitation
Regd. Office
Kadayara Building,
Chittattumukku
Kaniyapuram, Trivandrum

Sri Balachandran Nair
(President)
Non Residents Indian's Welfare Association
P.B. No. 6
Ambalapuzha P.O.
Alappuzha

THE PAYYANNUR GULF MENS WELFARE CO-OPERATIVE SOCIETY
No. C1115, P.O. Payyannur,
Kannur
670307

UNITY OF NON RESIDENT KERALITES
Subeir Shamsudheen
(Chairman)
Anil Bhavan
1400/XII, Y.M.C.A. Road
Alappuzha

VIDESHA MALAYALEE FELLOWSHIP
A.M. Madhusoodhanan
(President)
3/752, Anikkampoil
6th Mile, Kadirur, Kannur

WAYANAD DISTRICT PRAVASI SANGHAM
T.P. Prabhakaran
(Vice-President)
STED Sub Centre
Gudalai, Kalpetta

VIDESHA MALAYALEE ASSOCIATION
T.K.S. Babu, President
H.O. Aruvi Tourist Home,
Pattom Palace P.O. Trivandrum

WORLD MALAYALEE BUSINESS FORUM
V.V. Devasia
Ahanas Building
Ambadi Lane, Krishnaswami Road
Kochi-35

NON RESIDENT INDIANS AND RETURNEES WIDOWS WELFARE ASSOCIATION
D. Sudha Devi
(President)
'Kanakam', Ezhokone
Kollam-691505

NRIR-Experts and Professionals
G.P. Nair
Vaidyar A Salam
(Chief Promoters)
Megapbyte Royal Business Centre
Floor 5, Karimpanal Statue Avenue
Trivandrum-695001

NRIS' WELFARE ASSOCIATION (NWA)
T.P. Chakkunny
(Secretary)
XX/256 Poothole P.O.
Thrissur-4

PACHIMA KOCHI PRAVASI LABOUR CONTRACT CO-OPERATIVE SOCIETY LTD.
Antony Xavier
(Chief Promoter)
XI/1345, Odatha
Fort Kochi-682001

WORLD MALAYALEE ACADEMIC FORUM
Joy Plathottam
Ahanas Building, Ambadi Lane
Krishnaswami Road, Kochi-35

STATE RETURNED GULF MALAYALI'S ASSOCIATION
M.S. Hameed
Sainaba Manzil
Poovar, TVPM-695525

PRAVASI MALAYALEE COUNCIL (KALLARA MEKHALA)
A. Ali Akbar
(President)
Pravasi Bhavan, Thangal Building
Trivendrum-695608

PRAVASI SAMRAK SHANA SAMITHI (KERALA CHAMBER)
Dr. E.V. Sivan
(Vice-President, PSS)
Sankar Bhavan
S.M. Hospital Complex
Kadakkal P.O. Kollam

PRAVASI SANGHOM
Idukki District Committee
Gemini Tourist Complex
P.B. No. 22
Thodupuzha-685584

PRAVASI SANGHOM (ALAPPUZHA DISTRICT)
Sri K. Salim Rawthar
(President)
Thadathineth Saji Villa,
Kollakadavu Post

PATHANAMTHITTA DISTRICT PRAVASI SANGHAM
Sri Madhanamohan
(President)
Manesh Bhavan, Muthoor Post
Pathanamthitta

KOLLAM JILLA PRAVASI SANGHOM
Nazar Thittumoola
(President)
Near Upasana Hospital
Kollam-1

MARUNADAN MALAYALI EKOPANASAMITHI
Manoharan Nambron
(Convenor)
'Green Garden'
P.O. Pazhayangadi
Kannur-670358

KUWAIT PRAVASI ASSOCIATION
M.G. Varghese
(President)
Building No. XXVI/313
Pallikara, Thiruvalla

MALABAR CHARITABLE SOCIETY
Adv. K.M. Asharaf
(Chairman)
R.P. 10/400, Ettikulam P.O.
Ezhimala

MALABAR PRAVASI COUNCIL
E. Muhamad Haji
(President)
Mundappalam, Kondotty P.O.
Malappuram-673638

PRAVASI SANGHOM
Pravasi Bhavan
K.P. 8/288 Ullas Nagar
Peerorkada P.O.
Thiruvananthapuram-685584

NON RESIDENT INDIANS AND RETURNEES EMPLOYEES ORGANISATION
P. Subhash Chandra Bose
(President, State Committe)
Thulasi Mandiram, Ezhukone
Kollam-691505

NON RESIDENT INDIANS AND RETURNEES ORGANISATION (KARUNAGAPALLY TALUKA UNIT)
Jacob T. Vaidyan
(President), Non-Resident Indians and Returnees Organisation
Thengumvilayil, Thavalakkara
P.O. Kollam-690524

PRAVASI MALAYALEE COUNCIL
Koshi Joseph
(State President)
Pravasi Bhavan, Santhi Nilayam Bldg.
Amboori P.O.
Trivandrum-695505

PRAVASI MALAYALEE COUNCIL
Mr. Prasanna Kumar
(Dist. President)
Pravasi Bhavan,
Chathanoor Kollam

PRAVASI MALAYALEE FEDERATION
Vijayan Kuttiadi
(Gen. Secretary)
Thuvakkode, Chemancheri
Calicut-673304

GULF MALAYALI RETURNED ASSOCIATION
Ernakulam District Committee
K.M. Ibrahim
(Secretary)
Kallamthara, Pattanamkavala,
Vadakkekara, North Paravoor-683522

PRAVASI MALAYALI ASSOCIATION (RANNI UNIT)
Dr. Soman Kumar
(President)
St. Mary's Hospital
Karikulam P.O. Ranni
Pathanamthitta-689682

GULF MALAYALI RETURNS ASSOCIATION
S. Nissar
(Gen. Secretary)
Palliyude Padittathil
Chingoli P.O. Alappuzha-690532

KASARGOD DISTRICT PRAVASI SANGHAM
Sri Hassinar A. Thalangara
(President)
SAV Villa, Thalangara
Kasargod-671122

KERALA EX-LIBYAN EMPLOYEES ASSOCIATION
P.K.N. Kaimal
(President)
c/o Thayyi Tourist Home
Thathampalli P.O.
Alappuzha-688013

KASARGOD JILLA GULF RETURNEES & WELFARE ASSOCIATION
Ranindran Master
(Secretary)
Shukkoor Building
Kottachety, Kanhangad
Kasargod-671315

KERALA GULF PRAVASI SURAKSHA COUNCIL
Thundil Hassan
(President)
Thundil House, Krishnapuram-690533

MAVELIKKARA TALUKA OVERSEAS RETURNEES ASSOCIATION
B.P. IX/660
N.B. Buildings, Nambukulangara

NON RESIDENT INDIANS AND RETURNEES ASSOCIATION (POOVATHOOR UNIT)
S. Gopalakrishnan (President)
'Aswathy'
Poovathoor West, Mavady P.O.
691507

NIGERIA FRIENDS ASSOCIATION
V.G. Chacko
(President)
Vallimannil
Karuvankonam, Kowdiar
Trivandrum

Sri M.V. Salam Paravanna
c/o Malappuram Jilla Pravasi Sanghom
Jubily Road

NON RESIDENT INDIANS AND RETURNEES ASSOCIATION (STATE COMMITTEE)
Johnson Mathai

P.O. Kunnummel
Malappuram

(Chairman)
kannankara Puthenveedu
Puthoor P.O. Kottarakkara
Kollam-691507

GULF RETURNS ASSOCIATION
C. Ayyammu Haji
(Gen. Secretary)
Chettiyan Thodi House
Alanalloor P.O.
Mannarkad-678601

GULF RETURNEES AND EMPLOYEES ORGANISATION
V.T. Abdhul Koya Master
(Secy) Haseena Manzil, P.O.
Pokkunnu
Calicut-673013

GULF RETURNS ASSOCIATION MANNAR
V.A. Abdhul Rasheed
Padipurakkal Veedu
Kurattikad, Mannar P.O.
Alappuzha

GULF RETURNEES WELFARE CO-OPERATIVE SOCIETY LTD.
No.S. 307, Hosdurg,
Kanhangad
Kasargod

KANNUR DISTRICT PRAVASI SANGHOM
Sri T.P. Aravindakshan
(President)
'Ramayana' Pallikkunnu
Kannur-4

KALLAR MUSLIM JUMA ATH UAE PRAVASI ASSOCIATION
Rajapuram P.O.
Kallar, Kasargod Dist.
Kerala-671532

All India Gulf Returnees Association
Sharmila's
Lekshminada
Kollam-691014

Indo Arab Confederation Council
Regd. Office
Emirate Building, Kallai Road
Calicut-2

World Malayalee Council
Chennilode
Mecical College Post
Trivandrum

Sharjah Indian Association
c/o Sri Samuel P. George
(President)
Gil- Gal Plamootil, Pulimukku
Avaneeswaram, Kollam-17

Ex. Gulf Malayalee Association
Sree Ram Building
Poonkunnam
Thrissur-2

Pravasi Malayalee Council
Pravasi Bhavan
Thangal's Complex
C.H. Cross Road, Nadakkavu
Kozhikode-673001

Association of All Kerala Unemployed Gulf Returnees Rehabilitation

Non Residents Indian's Welfare Association
P.B. No. 6

Regd. Office
Kadayara Building,
Chittattumukku
Kaniyapuram, Trivandrum

Gulf Returnees Welfare
Association
Registered Office
BNRA 30
Balavan Nagar, Manacaud
Trivandrum-9

Kuwait and Gulf Returnees
Organisation
Beena Shopping Complex
Vembayam P.O.
Thiruvananthapuram-695615

Gulf Returnees Organisation
(GRO)
Regd Office
c/o Indianoor Hamsa
Indianoor, Kottakkal-676503

Gulf Malayalee Returned
Association
c/o Sri Achuthan Mavelikkara
(Gen. Secretary)
Panutharayil
Ponnezha, Thekkekara P.O.
Mavelikkara-7

Pravasi Malayalee Council
Shyamala Complex
1st Floor, Near Training School
Kannur-670002

Gulf Keralites' Welfare Association
c/o P.K. Kunheethutty
(President)
Alinchuvadu, Payyangadi
Tirur-676108

Ambalapuzha P.O.
Alappuzha

Pravasi Council
Pravasi Bhavan
Darussalam Complex
Thriprayar, Nattika P.O.
Thrissur-680566

Gulf Returnees Rehabilitation trust
c/o U.A. Khader Rawther
(Chairman)
Mullamangalam, Madathara
Kollam-691541

All Kerala Gulf Returnees
Association
'AKGRA'
c/o Dwimani
(President)
Baby Madom, Vakkom P.O.
695308

Non Resident Indians and
Returnees Organisation Gulf
Returnees welfare Association
c/o Jacob T.K. Vaidyan
(President)
Thengumvilayil
Thevalakkara P.O. Kollam-24

Gulf Keralites' Welfare Association
Regd. Office
Karthika Building,
Pallarimangalam P.O.
Mavelikkara-690107

Kairali Pravasi Association
Registered Office
ARA81, Devasam Board Junction
Kavadiyar P.O.
Trivandrum-3

Dheseeya Gulf Returnees
Organisation
'Nandavanam'
Thiruvallom P.O.
Thiruvananthapuram-695027

Samad Mankada
(President)
Pravasi Malayalee & Gulf Returns
Association
Mankada Area Committee
Mankada P.O. Malappuram
District
Kerala-679324

Abdhul Razak
(President)
Kerala Muslim Cultural Centre
Wayanad District Co-ordination
Committee
Kalpetta P.O.
673121

President
Wayanad District Pravasi Sangom
Near woodlands, Main Road
Kalpetta P.O. Wayanad-673121

V.P. Zuhra
(President)
Pravasi Malayali Vanitha Council
34/652A, Civil Station P.O.
Kozhikode-673020

K. Sasidharan
(President)
Kerala Gulf Returnees' Association
Chirayinkeezh,
Chirayinkeezh P.O.
695304
Thiruvananthapuram District

Najeeb
(Secretary)
Malappuram Sangam Pravasi
Sangam
Sted Sub Centre
Uphill, Malappuram

P.M.A. Azeez
(President)
Kasargod Jilla Gulf Returnees &
Welfare Association
Shukkoor Building
Kottachery P.O. Kanhangad
Kasaragod-671315

Kuwait Non Resident Keralites Un
compensation Beneficiaries Forum
Half Velluvambaram
Malappuram-673651

C.A. Muhammed Rafi
(President)
Non Resident Indians &
Returnees' Association
Mabrooq, Edamon P.O.
Punalor, Kollam District

T.P. Antony
(President)
Kerala Pravasi Sangamam
State Committee
15/14 Karuvelippadi
Cochin-682002

P.R. Kishore
(President)
Pravasi Accademy & Community
Development Society
Anakkayam, Anakkayam P.O.
Munduparambu (Via)
Malappuram District
676509

Subhas Chandra Bose
(President)
Non Resident Indians and
Returnees Employees Organisation
State Office
Near VSHS, Ezhukone Junction
Kollam-691505

P.M. Sethumadhava Menon
(President)
Kerala Pravasi (Returner's
Congress Council)
Malappuram District Committee
Kanhiramukku P.O.
Malapputam District 679584

P. Muhammad Shafi
(President)
Gulf Returnees Welfare
Association
State Committee
Thikkadappuram,
Neeleswaram
Kasaragod District

S. Ahammed
(President)
All Kerala Gulf Returnees
Organisation State Committee
Bismi,T.C. 35/1058
Gandhi Nagar, Vallakadav
Trivandrum-695008

Indianoor Hamsa
(President)
Federation of Foreign Returnees
Organisation
Lakshmi Nagar
E-2 Pattom Palace P.O.
Thiruvananthapuram-695004

Vidheesa Malayalee Cultural
Forum
c/o Mankulam Jayaprakash
(President)
Mangalapallil
Elampal P.O.
Punalur

Sajith Kumar
(Secretary)
Mother Theresa Memorial
Charitable Society
c/o Kollamvilakom
Chirayinkeezhu P.O.
Trivandrum District

George Abraham
(General Secretary)
Foreign Employed and Returned
Malayalis
(FERMA)
XXX/936, Appose Complex
Near YMCA
Pathanamthitta-689645

Chacka Ravi
(General Secretary)
All Kerala Pravasi Malayalee
Welfare Association
T.C 36/1074
West Fort
Trivandrum

M.P. Moideen
(General Secretary)
Kerala State Ex Gulf Welfare
Association
Kozhikode District Committee
League Centre
Kurial Lane
Kozhikode-673032

N.J. Satheesh Chandra Babu
(President)
All India Gulf Returnees Association
Kaithakode Unit
Santhi Bhavan, Kaithacodu P.O.
Kollam-691543

Gopalakrishnan S.
(President)
Non Resident Indians and Returnees Association
Aswathy
Poovattoor West, Mavady P.O.
691507

Index